MW00805253

The Literary Agent's Guide to Getting Published
and Making Money from Your Writing

Bill Adler, Jr.

CLAREN BOOKS
A DIVISION OF ADLER & ROBIN BOOKS, INC.

$14.95 U.S.

The Literary Agent's Guide to Getting Published
and Making Money from Your Writing

Bill Adler, Jr.

CLAREN BOOKS
A DIVISION OF ADLER & ROBIN BOOKS, INC.
www.clarenbooks.com
www.adlerbooks.com

The Literary Agent's Guide to Getting Published
and Making Money from Your Writing

Published by Claren Books
A Division of Adler & Robin Books, Inc.
   3000 Connecticut Avenue, N.W.
   Washington, D.C. 20008
   adlerbooks@adlerbooks.com
   http://www.adlerbooks.com
   http://www.clarenbooks.com

Printed in the United States of America. First Edition

Library of Congress Cataloging-in-Publication Data

Adler, Bill, Jr.
   The literary agent's guide to getting published : and making money
   from your writing / Bill Adler, Jr.
      p.   cm.
   ISBN 1-892025-00-0 (alk. paper)
   1. Authorship—Marketing Handbooks, manuals, etc.
   2. Authors and publishers Handbooks, manuals, etc. I. Title
   PN161.A37 1999
   808'.02—dc21   99-21349
                                                            CIP

Contents

The Guide That Editors Requested: An Introduction   1

Chapter One—Getting Ideas for Books   7

Chapter Two—Honing Your Writing Skills   21

Chapter Three—How to Write a Book Proposal   39

Chapter Four—How to Approach Publishers
and Agents   89

Chapter Five—About Query Letters   109

Chapter Six—Top Editors Tell What Makes a
Book Proposal Sell   131

Chapter Seven—The Questions Literary Agents
Are Most Often Asked   159

Chapter Eight—You Have a Book Publisher:
Now What?   171
    Negotiating Your Book Publishing Contract   171
    Book Writing Guidelines   174
    Promoting Your Book   176

Chapter Nine—Sample Book Proposals   181
    Your Second Pregnancy   182
    Business Wisdom From the Talmud   194
    Tell Me a Fairy Tale: A Parent's Guide to
      Telling Magical and Mythical Stories   217

Acknowledgments   235

About Bill Adler, Jr.   237

The Guide That Editors Requested:
An Introduction

I have been a literary agent for more than a decade. I co-own my agency, Adler & Robin Books, Inc., with my wife, Peggy Robin, where I work with a team of four other agents and two staff assistants. For most of the time that we've been in business we have given away a pamphlet to our clients entitled *The Literary Agent's Guide to Getting Published and Making Money from Your Writing*. Then one day I noticed that we were getting many requests for the guide from authors who were not our clients and from publishers, as well. Sometimes a publisher would ask for not one but several copies. Soon we realized we had produced a valuable document, one that we should share as widely as possible.

Now that is what we have done. By turning *The Literary Agent's Guide to Getting Published* into a book, we have done more than make it easily available to writers and other literary professionals— we have also expanded it into the most complete guide to writing book proposals you can find anywhere.

The Literary Agent's Guide to Getting Published is based on our knowledge and experience as agents for a collective total of more than fifty years. To give you, the reader, the broadest possible perspective, we have also drawn on a pool of authors, editors, and publishers for their best advice and insights.

While I have a good idea of what makes a proposal worth publishing—and what doesn't—I'm always learning. If I knew everything, publishers would never reject anything I send them (and unfortunately, sometimes they do). That's why I've included in this guide some tips and suggestions from publishers and editors that contradict some of my own suggestions. As you'll find out, publishing is very much a seat-of-the-pants business. Keep an open mind to the great variety of approaches and ideas advanced in this guide, try them out, and then stick with what works best for you.

That's been my own philosophy about this business. If a proposal works for me—if it strikes a chord with me, if it makes me sit up, or say, "What a dynamite book this would make!" then I'll push for its publication as hard as any agent can. Still, I realize that oftentimes even top-notch proposals get rejected. It's just one of those quirky things about the publishing world. There are lots of oddball reasons why book proposals get rejected. Here are a few:

- The editor is on his or her way out of a publishing house. Few editors are going to accept proposals right before they leave.
- All the slots for that particular book are filled. Publishers often have a few slots—or openings—for a particular type of book, and once they've contracted for a certain number of books in that category, they simply aren't going to accept any more.
- The publisher has just done a similar book. When I send out an author's proposal for *The Complete Book of Salamanders,* I hope the publisher who receives it does not already have a book in the works called *The World of Salamanders.* If he does, that means certain rejection, no matter how outstanding the proposal I'm representing.
- Similar books aren't selling well.
- The editor is simply too busy right now. No editor admits that, but it's a very common reason for rejecting proposals.

The only rule you need to remember to write a book proposal is that there are no hard and fast rules for writing a book proposal. If you are Leonardo DiCaprio and you decide to write your autobiography, a one-sentence proposal will suffice. If you have an idea about the history of fax machines, then you should count on writing a few dozen pages at least, including a representative sample from the book. Writing a book proposal isn't a mysterious process. In the chapters that follow, I'll walk you through the process step by step.

One useful fact to keep in mind at all times: Book proposals are written for *publishers,* not book buyers. Every remark you make should be addressed to the publisher, because it is the publisher who makes the decision to buy or reject your proposal. Any information that helps to persuade the publisher to buy your proposal should be included. Everything in your proposal should be designed to show the publisher how your book will attract and hold its audience—that is, how it will become a successful, money-making book. Anything that does not work to that end should be left out of the proposal.

In other words, a proposal is first of all a *sales tool.* Initially at least, the publisher is the market. You and your ideas are the product. Ultimately, book buyers are the market too, but remember, you've got to sell the proposal to a publisher first. If a paragraph helps to sell the proposal, include it. If it doesn't, hit the delete key.

There are two things a publisher will want to know before he or she is willing to risk time and money on you and your idea. The publisher must first be assured that book buyers are going to want your book; second, that your book is a more worthwhile project than some other book the publisher might do instead. Each new book costs a publisher thousands, or tens of thousands, of dollars to produce. Most of that money goes for printing and distribution; only a small fraction goes into the typical author's advance. Each new book must compete for attention in an increasingly crowded field: Around 50,000 new books were published in the United States last year. *About half of those lost money.* Those aren't good odds, so you must show the publisher why your book will beat the odds.

The first requirement for any proposal is that it must be well written. If you have any doubts about your writing abilities, work on that first. Chapter Two has much useful information to help you hone your writing skills. You might also benefit from reading a good writing guide. Peter Elbow's *Writing with Power* (Oxford University Press) and William Zinsser's *On Writing Well* (Harper Perennial) are two books worth having on your reference bookshelf.

Three Secret Weapons

Good, strong writing ability is just the beginning. Every proposal needs that little something extra to help it stand out from the crowd. Here are three secret weapons that will help you put together a successful proposal. Keep these principles in mind as you work on every aspect of your proposal.

Secret Weapon #1: Make your book fit into one category.

Visualize walking through a bookstore. Where would you find your book? In the humor section? In sociology? In self-help? In reference? Your book has to fit neatly into one or another category. Bookstore owners make ordering decisions based on the layout of their bookstore. That is, they have to consider how to shelve the books they order. They don't like confusion—it makes it difficult for customers to find books. If they see a book in the publisher's catalog that is, for example, a humorous look at sexual behavior, they see a problem: Where to shelve the book? Under Humor? Or Sexuality? The simplest solution, the bookstore owner might conclude, is not to order the book at all. The one category principle doesn't mean that your book can't combine two subjects; it just means that you need to emphasize only one of them when you pitch the book to the publisher, so that the publisher can do so when subsequently pitching the book to bookstores.

Secret Weapon #2: Make your book a must-buy for specialty markets.

Find a niche for your book that ordinary bookstores do not serve. The life of the average book in print is shorter than ten years, but books that serve a specialized market are more likely to stay in print for decades. Specialized outlets, such as catalogs and specialty stores, may keep ordering books long after interest has waned from traditional bookstores. In addition to catalogs and specialty stores, niche markets include specialty book clubs, on-line sales, television sales, direct mail, sales through magazine ads, and sales through organizations, religious institutions, and professional societies. The depth of interest in a book can often be measured by the number of people who participate in groups or ventures based on its subject. The more places you can specifically identify, and the more members that belong to the groups and outlets formed around an interest in your subject matter, the better your odds of selling the book to a publisher—and the better the publisher's odds of selling the book to consumers.

Secret Weapon #3: Keep the sales representative in mind.
The secret army in the book business is the publisher's sales force. These are the people who get bookstores, catalogs, and specialty stores to buy books. Without the sales force, your book would never get to consumers. It's also your book's sales representative who determines whether your book is sold spine out or face out. (A face out presentation is, of course, more likely to attract potential buyers.) A sales representative has about thirty seconds to convince a bookstore owner to carry a particular book. When you write your proposal, keep the sales representative in mind. What is that sales representative going to say in his or her thirty seconds of pitch time? If you can figure out what is the most effective selling line that can fit into that window of time, then you have the ideal opening paragraph for your book proposal.

CHAPTER ONE

Getting Ideas for Books

If It Sells, It Can Be a Book

I can't help you with novels—I will admit that up front. Same thing for children's books—because both adult fiction and children's literature must spring from the writer's own creative impulses. That is to say, you can't write a novel based on a market analysis of what sells…at least not a novel that would be worth reading. Fiction is seldom sold through proposals. Unless the fiction writer is already a household name, he or she is expected to have a completed work to show to a publisher.

What I can tell you is how publishers typically react to the new ideas for books that come to them in the form of a proposal. When it comes to nonfiction and computer books, *there* I have experience by the ream-load. Receiving and reviewing somewhere in the neighborhood of 5,000 queries and proposals per year, my agents and I have learned that it's not enough for an idea to be well presented. The idea needs to leap out at you, set off bells in your head, and tell you, "There's a great book waiting to be written about this subject!"

How do you recognize an idea that's worthy of a book-length treatment? To me the most reliable gauge comes in the form of sales of related products. I take a look at what's selling, what's "hot" in the business world, and I ask myself, has anyone done a book about this phenomenon? For example, I may notice that a particular piece of exercise equipment is flying out of the stores. Let's say it's an automatic jump rope machine. I see it advertised everywhere. Then, maybe one day I overhear someone on the subway chatting to a seatmate about how much they love the new exercise machine they've just bought. I can tell there's growing public interest, but can that interest be captured in a book? I start thinking up titles. *Auto-Jump Your Way to Health and Fitness? Jump for Your Life? The Complete Guide to Auto-Jump Machines?*

Next I might bounce my book idea off a few friends or associates whose judgment I trust. If they all say "yes," or "definitely," or anything else that's unequivocally positive, I know I've got a winner. In that case I get right to work on writing the proposal. But many times I'm asked, "Are you sure there's enough to fill out a book? Wouldn't this work better as a magazine article?"

Then I need to do a little more investigating before I hit the keyboard. I'll see whether there are computer chat groups that have been formed to discuss problems with the exercise equipment or how to structure a workout. I'll pick up sales brochures and see what the equipment promises its users. I will probably buy one and try it out myself. (The cost of the machine will ultimately be deductible from any taxes due on the earnings from the sale of my book.) I'll search for any magazine articles that have been published dealing with questions and problems that auto-jump machine users are experiencing. It may turn out that there were some important issues the magazine article didn't cover. New concerns, new possibilities may have sprung up since the equipment was last written about. I'll also look into whether there are any organizations, clubs, or specialty stores that might be interested in carrying a book on the auto-jump machine. The more information I uncover to show the public's interest, the better prepared I will be to create a book proposal compelling enough to make a publisher want to buy my book.

You also need to take into account your own areas of interest and expertise. I happen to be an exercise junkie. I work out an hour to two hours daily, and I have sufficient educational background in physiology and sports medicine to be able to research and write a book on a new piece of exercise equipment quickly and accurately.

You need to pick a subject that is both exciting and challenging for you to explore, but not beyond your ability to explain clearly to your readers.

Here's my formula: Public Interest multiplied by Product Sales, Advertising, Increasing Membership in clubs and organizations, plus Writer's Enthusiasm and Expertise equals Book Idea. PI × (PS + A + IM) + WE + E = !

Here is another possible application of the formula. You are a parent of an infant, and you've lately noticed that there's a growing variety of gourmet baby foods for sale on the supermarket shelves. You've seen a number of magazine articles discussing the proper diet for babies. You've heard quite a few conversations between friends about all the new choices there are in baby foods. You think: *Babies Taste Test: Rating the New Baby Foods,* or: *The Best for Your Baby: A Parent's Guide to Baby Food.*

You can think along these lines for any new product you see or trend you spot, anyplace you go. You're in a hardware store, and you find yourself coming up with ideas for new home renovation books. In your doctor's waiting room you see patient information pamphlets for new drugs, and books about health problems and their treatments spring to mind. Even when you're on vacation, you could be thinking up new book ideas—like a travel guide that would help people avoid the same booking mistakes you just made. You're at home working on the computer, and there's no end of books you can imagine that would help you and all those millions of other frustrated computer users like you: books to answer your questions about whatever program you're using, books about the on-line world, books about web site design—the possibilities are as limitless as cyberspace itself.

Go Beyond the Obvious

One of the tips I'll pass along now is to try not to focus on the very first book idea that pops into your head. With so many thousands of books published each and every year, you can be virtually certain that if it's an obvious idea, it's already been done. Try tackling your subject from just a little bit off-center, from an askew angle, if you can. Let's say you've noticed that vegetarian cuisine has become very popular lately. Whatever you do, *don't* propose another vegetarian cookbook. Almost any publisher of cookbooks that you approach will tell you they've already got one in print. But what about a nationwide guide to vegetarian restaurants and grocery stores? Some years back, we received a book proposal for a specialty cookbook about how to prepare festive vegetarian holiday fare. We sold the book, titled *'Tis the Season,* for a healthy sum, and many years later, it's still selling well.

Let me tell you how I have developed some of my own ideas. I'll start with this book—*The Literary Agent's Guide to Getting Published and Making Money from Your Writing.* As an agent, I found it useful to have on hand a short guide for my clients about how to write a book proposal. As a writer who once got paid by the word, I can attest to the fact that "short" is never long enough. To include all the information I wanted my authors to know, the booklet soon grew to more than fifty pages. Adler & Robin Books gave the guide away to all our potential clients, and then on a whim I sent it to several editors, and I told these editors that they could copy the guide and distribute it to their authors. Several editors did just that, and a few of them asked me for additional copies. "What's wrong with their copiers?" I wondered. It took me no time at all to figure out that the book was in demand. A book in demand means a book that will sell. In that case, why was I giving it out for free?

But my favorite story about coming up with a book idea is how I came to write my biggest-selling book, *Outwitting Squirrels: 101 Cunning Stratagems to Reduce Dramatically the Egregious Misappropriation of Seed from Your Birdfeeder by Squirrels.* (Originally, I had entitled the book *Outwitting Mr. Squirrel,* until I realized, upon closer examination of squirrels, that the title made a very gender-incorrect assumption. But I digress.)

I didn't start out as a birdfeeding enthusiast. In fact, in New York City where I grew up, I hardly ever saw a bird—besides a pigeon, that is—and who would want to feed pigeons? They're little more than flying rats. But then I moved to Washington, D.C. I decided I wanted a pet—a cat or a dog or something like that. The apartment building I lived in had a rule against pets, so a friend of mine, Stephanie Faul, suggested putting up a birdfeeder. Enjoy the color and antics of animals without having to clean up the mess, she said. Or take them for long walks on rainy days, I thought to myself. Okay, I said, it's worth a try.

So one day I attached a clear, rectangular feeder to my window with suction cups. I added a dash of sunflower seeds and watched and waited. Nothing. But the next day—ah ha! There was, not a bird, but a squirrel in my feeder. And not just at my feeder, but actually *in* my feeder. This squirrel had squeezed himself into my ten-inch long feeder and was using it not only as a snack bar, but as a couch, too. I banged against the window and that frightened the squirrel away. For a little while. Later the squirrel appeared again, and he (or she) quickly learned that there was a piece of solid glass between me and it, and no matter how hard I banged, I was not going to go through that glass. I was infuriated with this squirrel and would frequently scream at it whenever it invaded my feeder. Unfortunately, I would often scream "Get the #%@$!#$& out of here!" while I was on the telephone; this sharply cut into my social life. Like many people with a deep, troubling problem I sought consolation in books and support groups. While I discovered that there were plenty of "support groups"—by which I mean birdfeeder clubs—I found no books about my problem. That, more than anything else, was shocking to me as a writer. A big problem with no books on the subject! That's everything an author could want.

I immediately sprang into action. I had no trouble finding a wealth of information. One of the first facts I learned was that birdfeeding is a multibillion-dollar business. While it seems that every business is a billion-dollar business, I also discovered that bird feeders have tremendous passion when it comes to their hobby. Almost universally, people who feed birds absolutely *loathe* squirrels.

I took a step back from my new hobby, birdfeeding, and looked at it from the perspective of a potential publisher: If millions of people feed birds, and most of these people are passionate about defending their feeders from squirrels, and there is currently no book dedicated to the bird feeder's war against the squirrel, then there must be a tremendous opportunity for a book to fill the niche.

There was only one problem with this idea: Most publishers are in New York City and understand as much about birdfeeding—not to mention squirrels—as I did before I got started in this pursuit. Remember what I've said about having to convince a *publisher,* as opposed to consumers, to buy your book. Well, I sent out twenty proposals to all the major New York publishers and soon got back twenty rejections. I was disappointed but not terribly surprised. The twenty-first publisher I chose was Chicago Review Press, in the Midwest—where there are lots of birds. There must have been someone on the editorial committee who fed birds, too, and who understood how much my book was needed. With the publisher's enthusiastic "Yes!" plus an $800 advance, I was off and writing. A year later my book was in print and the orders started flowing in from bookstores, birdfeeding stores, and wildlife catalogs all over the country. More than 250,000 copies later, the book is still doing well, and the royalty checks keep coming.

In a way, you could say it was chance that I happened to mention my petless status to a friend who fed birds. But chance had nothing to do with my investigation of the birdfeeding market. Because I'm a writer who focuses on the market (rather than a writer who writes simply to express my own thoughts and feelings), I was able to turn my personal interest into a salable book. I asked the question, what specific birdfeeding problem can I find a way to solve that hasn't already been addressed in a book? What book do bird-lovers *need* badly enough to pay ten or fifteen dollars for?

If I had not been so market oriented, I might have spent a lot of time writing poetry about the beauty of the birds that came to my feeder—or perhaps venting my anger at the squirrels who would deny them their sunflower seeds. I might be very satisfied with the rhythm and grace of my words on the page, but you can bet any amount of money my work wouldn't be in print today, unless, of course, I paid to be self-published. But the point of this guide is to help you get published *successfully,* and that means you will be *paid* for your writing, not have to pay someone else to put your work in book form.

One group that's always looking for advice is the new parent market. Every year thousands of adults join this category of our population, and every year the majority of them find themselves baffled by the things their adorable little babies do that they hadn't expected. How to deal with colic? What about diaper rash? What if breastfeeding isn't as simple and easy to learn as you'd been led to believe? Like most new parents, my wife and I had these and thousands of other questions, but we're among the few that have managed to profit from being bewildered by our babies. We both ended up writing several books apiece out of our experiences.

My first parenting book grew out of a Sunday brunch with our then eight-month-old daughter, Karen. She was just at the babbling stage and delighted in naming everything she saw, in between gobbles of mushed-up food. We couldn't understand a word she said. "If only there were a dictionary to translate for parents," I said aloud. From that random thought came the proposal for *Baby-English: A Dictionary for Interpreting the Secret Language of Infants.* The first editor I sent it to was herself the mother of a babbling baby. She got the idea at once, and so came the book contract, and within a few months after that, the finished book.

Another successful book idea came from a common parenting travail. About five years ago, when Karen was two years old, I started to tell her bedtime stories. The only problem was that I couldn't remember how any of the usual fairy tales ended. So I would make up an ending, rewriting the Goldilocks script with details and events I knew would tickle Karen's fancy, sometimes trying to reinforce certain ideas I wanted my child to learn. In my version of the story, at the end a very sleepy Goldilocks toddles home from the bears' house and climbs into her own little crib and falls fast asleep. (Karen, however, seldom took the hint.) My wife, who's much more literate than I am when it comes to classic children's literature, didn't know the real ending to Goldilocks either. As we discussed other fairy tales, we realized that while we knew the names of many of the traditional tales, we didn't remember them well enough to tell them to Karen. There were plenty of anthologies of fairy tales we could have bought to read to her, but we wanted to be story*tellers,* adding our own touches. By freeing ourselves to change the story, we were able to drop some scary parts, change the sexism of the story (for example, by making Rapunzel more active in her own escape), and embroider in details we knew Karen would like, making the bedtime ritual much more enjoyable for all of us.

It didn't take long for me to realize that other parents might be interested in learning to tell stories to their children as I'd been doing for Karen. That was the genesis of *Tell Me a Fairy Tale: A Parent's Guide to Telling Magical and Mythical Stories.* Again, coming up with this idea was a combination of market analysis plus my own experience with a problem and inspiration about a solution.

As Karen grew, she acquired the *sine qua non* of toddlerhood: ear infections. Despite numerous visits to the pediatrician, I still felt like a novice when it came to them. With each ear infection I had more questions. (Not least of which was, "Why is Karen getting yet another ear infection?") Other parents, too, had plenty of ear infection questions. I found myself combing the Internet, looking for answers. I found dozens of chat groups anxiously searching for help, just as I was. We passed each other tips and furiously debated remedies. You can see where this is leading: I developed the idea for a question and answer book on childhood ear infections called *The Parents' Absolutely Complete Guide to Ear Infections.* Once again, personal experience and market analysis produced a book that is still in demand.

While no book can tell an unimaginative person how to come up with an idea, *The Literary Agent's Guide to Getting Published* is intended to help you recognize those ideas that can be developed into books. I think it is particularly worthwhile to note that in each of these cases I took a subject that had already been written about extensively—birdfeeding, fairy tales, and children's medical problems—and approached the problem from a different perspective, a side view. Take a popular subject and ask yourself, what is an off-center way of looking at it? What special spin can you throw on your subject? For example, nobody needs (and probably no publisher wants) another book about pregnancy, because there are already so many big ones on the bookstore shelves, competing for buyers. How can you redirect attention so that readers are getting new and different information—help they can't get from any other book on the bookstore's shelves (or any book they already own).

I was always envious of the writers who came up with *What to Expect When You're Expecting.* What a brilliant idea, to write about pregnancy not from the obstetrician's dry, medical perspective (that had already been done many times), but from the point of view of an experienced and helpful older friend, one who has had babies herself and can tell you what it felt like. Then I stopped and thought, "Is there anyone this book has left out?" After a brief study of the question I realized that the book was speaking almost exclusively to first-time mothers, women who had never experienced pregnancy before. But what about women pregnant with their second child? What about a book that could answer *their* questions: Will it feel the same as the first time around? What if it doesn't? How might it feel different? Are there any problems more common in subsequent pregnancies than in first ones? So I came up with the idea for *Your Second Pregnancy: What's Different This Time.* (And in case you're wondering, the answer is no, I didn't write it myself. After selling a publisher on the idea for the book, I found a good writer and mother of two to research and write the book.)

As I progress through the middle and later stages of parenthood, I'm sure I'll find other, more challenging parenting problems around which a book is just begging to be written. I'm actually looking forward to the teenage years: They hold out the prospect of virtually limitless topics to be addressed. My motto is there's always room for one more book—as long as it comes from a new perspective. The trick is to be open to seeing things from that fresh angle.

Grab the "Ah-ha Moment"

Different people keep their minds open to new ideas in different ways. You have to know yourself well to recognize when you are most receptive to a new way of looking at things. Do your best ideas come to you while you're deep in alpha-wave television viewing? Do ideas pop into your head during meals? While you're jogging? Just as you're dozing off to sleep?

You also need to ask yourself when you get your *best* ideas (as opposed to when you get any ideas at all). You may come up with plenty of ideas while watching kids' television programs with your children, but are these really good ideas? Or do you develop better ideas when you are taking a long, solitary walk in the woods (and don't happen to have a pen)?

I get a lot of good ideas while bicycling, which I do every day for ten to fifteen miles. Because it's hard to jot down ideas while cycling, I now carry a digital voice recorder—one of those card-sized electronic tape recorders that can be used easily and quickly. I also carry one in my car—another place where it's hard to write. You should always be ready to write down or record your ideas. You can always evaluate the merits and marketability of your ideas later, but if you lose your idea, well, then that's that. You *might* get your idea back, but even if you do, you may have lost the spark of the original. (I do not subscribe to the school of thought that goes like this: If it was a good idea, you'll remember it no matter what. That seems to me about as likely as thinking that you'll be able to retrieve your briefcase after you've left it somewhere in Grand Central Station.)

If you'd like to kick-start your own idea-generating processes, I definitely recommend Roger von Oech's *A Whack on the Side of the Head: How to Unlock Your Mind for Innovation* (Warner Books).

I am convinced that great book ideas can strike you anywhere, anytime—if only you keep your mind limber enough to catch them and do the necessary legwork (the research and organizing of material) to put them down in proposal form.

One successful author, Larry Kahaner (who has a sample proposal later in this book), has this to say about developing book ideas:

My book ideas come from slow analysis punctuated by lightning fast "Ah-ha's!"

I've been a journalist for more than twenty years, and I've developed a pretty good instinct for trends. After reading and hearing bits and pieces about a subject or idea, it becomes clear that there's something going on. The topic is on people's minds but not quite in the forefront.

This was the case with my latest book, *Competitive Intelligence,* published by Simon & Schuster. Let me explain that competitive intelligence is the legal and ethical method by which companies collect information about their competitors and the marketplace in general and turn that information into actionable intelligence. It's not industrial espionage.

The factors I saw contributing toward the growth of CI were the following:

The end of the Cold War. Suddenly, spies were out of jobs. How could they turn their collection and analysis skills to work in the private sector? Competitive intelligence.

The growth of the Internet, which has us thinking about how information is gathered and disseminated. There's so much information that it's become a commodity, a raw material, almost worthless until we take that information, filter it, and analyze until it becomes intelligence—something we can use to make decisions. That's CI.

Multinational companies like Motorola, Proctor & Gamble, Kodak, and Coca-Cola were quietly developing their CI departments. Not much was being written about it.

The globalization of business was proceeding more quickly than predicted. Companies needed a method to grow new markets, stay competitive worldwide, and learn about new competitors who seemed to come out of nowhere. CI was the answer.

Once I saw the big picture I started to make phone calls and search databases to confirm my belief in the trend. It became clear that I was on the right track. My agent and publisher thought so, too.

Competitive Intelligence is selling very well, with foreign rights sold to the U.K., Korea and Japan. I've become an expert on the subject and consult with companies and organizations on how to develop and implement CI programs. I've been asked to give speeches in the U.S. and overseas.

My best advice for developing book ideas is to read, read, and then read some more. Let yourself be open to new ideas.

Once you've had your "Ah-ha!" (as Larry Kahaner puts it), your next task is to find a way to translate the realization that a book needs to be written into the words and sentences that make up a book proposal. You need to know that when you write, you will capture the reader's attention. The best idea in the world will be wasted if it is badly expressed.

If you already know you can write cleanly and concisely (because you have been told you can by others who make their living evaluating and publishing prose—not because you simply have told yourself you're good), you may skip the next chapter and go straight to Chapter Three about how to write a book proposal.

All others will want to read Chapter Two for some easy-to-absorb tips about style, grammar, and format.

Saving Your Ideas

As a writer I often fret about where my data might go when I'm not looking. Ever since I was a boy and heard about friends' school papers that were eaten by their dogs, I've been worried about losing my valuable words. Even more so in the electronic age, where entire manuscripts are at the mercy of notional operating systems and fragile hard disks.

Backing up your work is as important as creating it. It's always a good idea to print your drafts now and then. There's nothing like a hard copy of your manuscript—unless you own a dog with a fondness for laser printer paper. But most of us don't print drafts daily (it goes against our environmental grain). If you don't print copies of your work, then it's a very good idea to back up your work to some removable media such as a Zip Disk or a removable hard drive such as a Jaz Drive. There's good software available that automates backups.

My motto about backing up is. "Only backup those things you can't afford to lose."

There are two kind of computer users: Those who have lost files and those who will.

Recently, I've started to use an offline backup service called @Backup. Off-line backups have several advantages over traditional disk backups: If there's a catastrophe—such as a fire in your house—a virus that kills your files, or if your computer is stolen, your data is perfectly safe. Off-site backup also lets you retrieve your data from anywhere. I like @Backup because it's easy to use, the data is encrypted, and it's inexpensive. In fact, @Backup is *much* easier to use and more automated than most tape or disk backup programs. @Backup stores multiple redundant copies of your files, so you can even retrieve earlier versions of what you've written. I like @Backup so much that we've decided to sponsor a page for them in this book. You can find out more about @Backup at www.adlerbooks.com/backup and on page 243.

CHAPTER TWO

Honing Your Writing Skills

Classes, Guides, Computer Programs: How Well Do They Work?

The trouble with most neophyte writers is that they believe that writing is an art. They think the important thing is to exercise creativity. They're wrong, at least as far as the normal practice of nonfiction writing is concerned. If you're talking about a Shakespeare, a Milton, or one of the Brontës, then yes, you *are* talking about art. But if you're talking about the kind of writing that most publishers are looking for, in a book that will sell in a hotly competitive market, then forget any thoughts of artistry; and start thinking about the *business* of writing. As in the case of anyone about to enter a new business, the key is to master the skills. Learn the craft—which in this case means learning how to say what you have to say, clearly and efficiently. Readers like to get to the point—that's what ten-plus years in this business has taught me about what makes a nonfiction book worth the buyer's hard-earned buck.

President Clinton won his first election by recognizing the main point of interest to the voters: "It's the economy, stupid." I think writers are successful when they recognize that, as far as readers of nonfiction are concerned, "It's the substance, stupid." It's what the book is *about* that's important. Make the reader understand the subject matter; don't fool around with rhetorical flourishes, trying to impress with style. Say what you have to say, then shut up.

Unfortunately, what I've just said is rarely taught in college-level writing courses. Instead, all too often, students learn just the opposite: that arty effects are a sign of talent, that the important thing is to express your individuality, that an essay full of complex sentences, embellished with similes and metaphors, is superior to writing that's brief and direct.

Publishers of books today certainly don't feel that way. The longer the book, the more it costs the publisher to produce. So if the same meaning can be packed into fewer pages, the publisher will save money. Besides, if the writer rambles on too long, readers will feel they're paying for a lot of padding and not enough substance. Better for a book to be a little bit too short; that way readers will figure the writer still has more to say on the subject, and they'll buy the writer's subsequent books.

Although too many writers come out of creative writing classes worse than they went in, I'm not against all types of writing classes. The one type of class I do recommend is a journalism class. Most journalism teachers still emphasize the old Five W's Rule. From the very first paragraph the objective is to tell the Who, What, Where, When, and Why. Of course, you may fall into a class in the "New Journalism"—a stylistic movement that's actually about three decades old—that believes in getting away from the basics and allowing the reporter to develop a personal style and employ artistic effects. You know you're reading a "New Journalism"-influenced piece in the newspaper when you've read the headline, the subhead, and all the way to the "jump," and you still haven't figured out what the piece is about. The way to avoid "New Journalism"-oriented classes is to ask the teacher for the reading list for the class in advance of signing up. If you see any works by Tom Wolfe, Daphne Merkin, or Joyce Maynard, keep looking for a different class.

Journalism classes may be offered at local colleges and universities, community colleges, adult education centers, or writers' organizations. Also keep an eye out for writers' workshops, seminars, and retreats. As with classes, you will need to find out in advance something about the teacher's view of the function of the class. If the purpose of the workshop or retreat is to encourage creativity and self-expression, you may not come away with anything of practical value to you in producing a salable book. My advice is to stay away from any course labeled "Creative Writing." It's a phrase most attractive to amateurs, diarists, and poets (few of whom ever make money).

If you haven't got the time or money for classes, you might do as well by reading a few good books about the writer's craft. Any writer will benefit from the classic "little book," *The Elements of Style* by William Strunk, Jr. and E. B. White (Macmillan). It's been in print in one version or another since 1935 and will probably remain in print forever, because it so clearly lays out the main principles of good writing. The advice doesn't become dated, because in every era readers appreciate clarity, directness, and correct form.

On the other hand, you might go for an up-to-the-minute writing guide, *The Complete Idiot's Guide to Grammar and Style,* put out by the makers of a popular series of computer help books. This reference work mimics the look of tech-support manuals with frequent use of boxed tips, lists of dos and don'ts, and loads of cartoons, diagrams, and other eye-catching features.

I also recommend three longer, more serious books about what makes for readable prose: William Zinsser's *On Writing Well* (Harper Reference), Jacques Barzun's *Simple and Direct* (University of Chicago Press), and Peter Elbow's *Writing with Power* (Oxford University Press).

An indispensable reference is *The Chicago Manual of Style* (The University of Chicago Press), which is the ironclad rulebook of grammar and usage of a great many publishing houses (perhaps the majority). If *The Chicago Manual of Style* forbids a usage, the writer must change the sentence (or leave it the way it is at his or her peril).

I have mixed feelings about the kind of writing assistance you can get from computer software designed to analyze and improve your writing. Most of the programs I've seen are no substitute for a real-life editor. There are times when a good writer needs to bend the rules of grammar, but the programs just can't deal with exceptions. On the other hand, they are good for helping a writer to break certain bad habits. If, for example, you tend to use a lot of clichés in your writing, then run a style analyzer program and let it highlight every cliché it finds. Don't, however, be tempted to let the program choose the substitute word or phrase for you. You need to work on coming up with your own non-clichéd means of expression and not hand off your responsibilities as a writer to some geeky computer programmer in Silicon Valley.

I feel the same way about spellcheckers. By all means, run the program after you're done with your document, but then be sure to check it yourself before you send it out. Spellcheckers, if not backed up by the human eye (and brain), can introduce as many errors as they eliminate. You may have heard of the famous story about the writer whose computer program suggested replacing the term "black" with the term "African-American." The writer clicked "OK" and the computer globally searched and replaced every usage—resulting in a sentence in the completed manuscript that described a bruise that had turned "African-American-and-blue."

Of course you should also be aware that computer spellcheck programs may leave many other types of errors uncaught. If you type "her" when you meant "here," the computer won't spot the mistake, because "her" is a correct word in itself. Only a human reader can root out those mistakes. If you send out a manuscript or a book proposal with a number of jarring errors because you haven't bothered to reread your own work after running a spellcheck, your potential publisher will conclude that you are a sloppy writer whose work will require extra hours of extremely careful editing. That's an expense most publishers will be happy to forgo by passing on your book idea.

General Principles of Good Writing for All Occasions

Know the ground rules of good writing. That means: learn to punctuate correctly; avoid run-on sentences; know when to start a new paragraph; know which words should be capitalized and what phrases should be italicized; and follow all the basic rules laid out in any mainstream stylebook. Once you have confidence that you know how to write standard English, you'll be able to recognize those rare situations in which the rules may be broken to good effect.

Organize your thoughts before you begin writing. Many writers find it helpful to make an outline of what they intend to write. That way you develop your ideas in logical sequence, starting with a simple premise that everyone accepts, then building upon it with the next thought, substantiated by the evidence you introduce that supports the next idea, which you substantiate by more evidence, and so on and so on until you arrive at your logical conclusion—at which point you stop. Outlining the whole of your piece (whether it is an article, a book proposal, or a complete book) keeps you disciplined. When you follow an outline, you will not end up repeating information that will later need to be cut, nor will you assume the reader knows a fact not yet introduced or substantiated. Even if you choose not to create a detailed outline of your work, you should always have at the very least a firm grasp of what information you plan to introduce, and in what order, before you start writing.

Write in your natural voice. Don't copy someone else's style, no matter how much you might admire that writer. Don't write in the style you think is expected of writers published in a particular journal or by a particular publishing company. This is especially true about academic writing. Far too many professors believe their writing needs to be as verbose and jargon laden as possible to be published in an academic journal. In fact, the best writing by professors is done by those who can make their ideas intelligible to laypeople, who use ordinary vocabulary to explain their work. Think of Carl Sagan (*Cosmos* and many other books), Freeman Dyson (*Disturbing the Universe*), Edward O. Wilson (*Consilience*). They're not just respected scientists—they're fine writers as well. Their success outside the academy comes because they are able to make their points clear to the book-buying public at large. The rewards they've reaped have been commensurate with their writing talent as much as with their scientific brilliance.

Choose the simplest, most direct way to express your thoughts. When you find yourself writing long complicated sentences, stop and rewrite. Break multiclause sentences into separate ones. Find the main subject and the main verb and bring them closer together. Eliminate adjectives and adverbs as much as possible. Instead, look for verbs that convey the nuances you want. For example, write "the police officer commanded," instead of "the police officer stated in a commanding tone of voice."

Read your writing aloud. If you find yourself stumbling over the reading of your words, then your writing isn't flowing well, and you should rewrite any sentences that tripped you up. Whenever you find it awkward to speak aloud any words or phrases that you had thought read all right on paper, rethink the phrasing. Address your audience on paper as if you were talking to a new acquaintance, someone who isn't familiar with you or your ideas, but who is intelligent and open-minded. You want to win over your audience, so keep your tone friendly and your arguments gentle; don't be combative or sarcastic. Assume basic fairness plus a little curiosity, but don't assume any special expertise. Don't overload your reader with specialized terms; but on the other hand, don't talk down to your reader by oversimplifying your points. If you're not sure whether you've hit the right note, then go for an impartial outsider's opinion (not your spouse or anyone else who may be obliged to spare your feelings).

Avoid the passive voice. I wish every writer who ever mailed me a book proposal would memorize this rule! "Jane was struck and her life extinguished by a single blow of a hammer wielded by Frank," writes a would-be author of a true crime book. If only he'd written, "Frank killed Jane with a single hammer blow," I'd have had confidence in his ability to tell the story, and I would have kept on reading. Instead, I tossed his proposal in the trash can. (Notice I didn't say, "His proposal was deposited in the waste receptacle by me")—which leads me to my next point.

Choose plain, short words over fancy, multi-syllabic ones. Never write "waste receptacle" when you're talking about a trash can. Never say "precipitation activity" when you mean "rain." Now, if you've picked the longer term because it's vague enough to cover several possibilities—rain, sleet, snow, freezing rain—and you don't know which form is expected, you are not gaining anything by hiding under the verbiage. Either tell the reader straight out that you don't know, or investigate further until you can say with precision whatever you were not initially sure about.

Don't get bogged down by the rules. You'll notice I ended the previous paragraph with a preposition. I know the rules of grammar, and I am fully aware of the editor's dictum that no sentence should ever end with a preposition. But I also know and follow a more important rule, which is that writing needs a certain flow and natural rhythm. If I rewrote the sentence "correctly" I'd have to write "...until you can say with precision whatever it was about which you were not initially sure." Not only is that awkward—it's all but unintelligible. As Winston Churchill once mockingly replied to a pedantic editor, "This is the sort of grammatical nonsense up with which I shall not put!" On the other hand, if you can find a simple and graceful way to rewrite a sentence and still observe the niceties of grammar, by all means, do so.

After the First Draft

If you apply the principles discussed above, your first draft should be basically well organized, say what you meant for it to say, and sound good to the ear when read aloud. But it can always be better. Every writer needs to go over his or her work with a critical eye, looking for inconsistencies, awkward sentences, unsubstantiated assertions, rough transitions between paragraphs or sections, and, of course, errors in typing, spelling, and grammar.

Never assume that an editor will take over these tasks for you once your proposal has been accepted. Unless you learn to produce clear and virtually error-free prose, odds are good you will never find a publisher in the first place. An editor's time is a precious commodity; one increasingly common way for publishers to cut down on costs is to accept only those book proposals and manuscripts that need minimal professional editing.

If you are unsure of your ability to edit your own work, then you need to have your work gone over by someone who knows good writing and whose comments you can be sure will not be biased by friendship, marriage, or family relationships. For some writers, the only way to get such reliable service is to hire a freelance editor. Others have colleagues or associates they can turn to, or friends who are willing to be brutal when necessary. I usually let my wife mark up my first drafts. She can be very critical (sometimes even snide), but I've learned that a writer should never take editing personally. Of course, we sometimes have a *professional* disagreement—but we're careful not to let that affect our home life.

After the first edit and round of rewriting you may want to run the piece by yet another outsider for an opinion and do still another round of correcting and polishing. You can, of course, go overboard with this process, ending up never satisfied, doing draft after draft— so you do need to know when to quit. A writer really should have some kind of internal clock set to ring at the right point—or a little voice that you hear telling you it's time to put your pencils down and pass your papers to the front of the room. Once you're satisfied that you've done the very best job that you can do with your article or proposal, put all your qualms and second guesses out of your head, send the work off, and pray. Agonizing beyond that point will only make you miserable, and writing should be one of the more enjoyable professions to pursue.

Two Writing Exercises

Exercise #1: Giving Directions
One of the most useful things a writer can learn how to do is give clear directions for a complicated task. Any writer of a self-help manual, cookbook, computer book, diet book, health book, or almost any sort of guide is basically writing a how-to. All writers of these types of books should try out the following exercise:

Give written directions only—no pictures or diagrams allowed— telling a person how to tie a shoelace. It's harder than you think. Of course, you could *show* someone in five seconds how to do it. But when people buy a book hoping to learn a new skill, it's usually because they don't have anyone available to show them in person how it's done. If you can accurately and concisely describe the steps a person has to take to tie a simple shoelace bow, you will probably be able to describe other actions of similar complexity, and write the sort of how-to book consumers will find helpful and will recommend to their friends.

Exercise #2: Finding the Point

A good way to learn to cut verbiage from your own writing is to take a shot at other people's worst. Here is a trio of real life examples. Try to find the smallest number of words to convey the same meanings for each of the four statements quoted below. (You don't need to rewrite any explanatory remarks that may precede the quoted statement.)

A. "I am reluctant to effectuate economics through the closing of schools, even for one day. I also have a question about the legality of such action."

—Irving Anker, Chancellor of
New York City public schools, 1975

B. When a reporter asked Nelson Rockefeller if he thought he'd win the presidential nomination at the 1976 Republican convention, he replied, "I cannot conceive of any scenario in which that could eventuate."

C. When asked if he was actively seeking the presidency in 1980, California Governor Jerry Brown gave this answer: "My equation is sufficiently complex to admit of various outcomes."

The answers are at the end of this chapter.

Seven Common Writing Problems and Their Solutions

Problem #1: Weakling Words

The column on the left is made up of problem words and phrases. These terms tend to weaken sentences. They can make writing vague, namby-pamby, pompous, or misleading. The column on the right is made up of stronger, shorter terms to use instead.

Problem Words and Phrases	Problem-Solving Words
at this point in time	now
during the preceding 24 hours	yesterday
it is our opinion	we believe
in close proximity to	near
in the majority of instances	usually
obtain an estimate of	estimate
on the occasion of	when
a total of twenty-eight	twenty-eight
in numerous instances	often
provide a summary of	summarize
came to the conclusion that	concluded
in the field of mathematics	mathematics
will have an impact on	will affect
in the normal course of events	normally
made a statement to the effect that	said
gave an untruthful statement	lied

Problem #2: Redundancies

A phrase contains a redundancy when one word of the phrase repeats the meaning of another. The classic example is "free gift." If you have to pay for something, then it's not a gift. Other redundancies to avoid include:

future goals	fully complete
revert back to	downtown city center
oral conversation	rural farm

baby lamb (also: baby duckling,
   male bull, female cow,
    and so on)
design concept

major masterpiece
personal friend
sad tragedy

Problem #3: Qualifiers and Space Fillers

Unless you're a politician intent on hedging your position, you will want to avoid words that water down your writing or fill up space without adding meaning. Words to use sparingly include:

somewhat
quite
rather
very
for the most part
indeed
thus (and especially, thusly)

actually
I would venture to say
it seems to me
as it were
if you will
as you may be aware
one would think*

Problem #4: Noun-Verb Agreement

Nothing will convince an editor that you're semiliterate faster than a few bad errors in noun-verb agreement. Singular nouns take singular verbs and plural nouns take plural verbs—seems simple enough, doesn't it? Things get more complicated, however, as sentences get longer and modifying phrases creep in between the subject and the verb.

> The advisory council of college students warns against drinking on campus.

The verb must be the singular "warns" to agree with its subject, "council," which is one entity—therefore singular. The modifying

---

*Avoid using "one" when you mean the typical person. Use "you" instead. It's more direct, and besides, "one" is primarily a British usage that sounds stilted to most American ears.

phrase "of college students" ends with a plural noun, but that doesn't change the singular nature of the subject of the sentence.

When you find yourself confused about whether to use a singular or plural verb, it's frequently because there are too many words separating the subject and its verb.

> The majority of the people who voted for lower taxes doesn't believe that bigger government is better government.

Sounds awful, doesn't it?—but it's grammatically correct. "Majority" is a singular noun. Shorten the sentence to eliminate the modifying phrase "of the people who voted for lower taxes," and you'll see what I mean:

> The majority supports a tax cut on the principle that smaller government is better government.

That sounds better. Another way to fix the sentence would be by eliminating the troublesome singular word "majority" and substituting a simpler, plural word, "most":

> Most of the people who voted for lower taxes believe in smaller government.

Problem #5: Dangling Modifiers
You don't have to understand grammatical terms such as "participial phrase" or "adverbial phrase" to know a dangling modifier when you see one. Just envision the literal meaning of this sentence:

> I saw him coming out of the corner of my eye.

Unless you meant to give your reader the impression that you are looking at yourself in the mirror and seeing a tiny person, about the size of a teardrop emerging from the corner of your eyeball, you had better plan to rewrite. You must move the troublesome phrase closer to the noun it is modifying (in this case, "I").

> Out of the corner of my eye I saw him coming.

Often dangling participles are unintentionally hilarious.

> A. Needing a brake job, I returned the car to the dealer.
>
> B. This new tape player is terrific. Weighing a mere ten ounces, the inventor has packed lots of sophisticated features into the system.

Can you rewrite them to un-dangle the modifying phrase? Answers are at the end of this chapter.

Problem #6: Missing Antecedents

"Antecedent" is the grammatical term for the noun that a pronoun has replaced. All too often in the writing samples that authors send me, I find myself wondering what an antecedent was meant to be. In the example below, the writer has written a string of sentences about problems in a city's recycling program. His concluding sentence contains a pronoun with an unclear antecedent:

> Magazines with staples in them jam up the sorting machines. Glass bottles are not being separated by color. Non-recyclable plastic bottles are thrown in with recyclable ones. This makes the system too labor-intensive to be cost-effective.

"This?" I wonder. "What's 'this'?" The last problem described? Or all three problems, taken together as one big problem in material sorting? Or perhaps "this" refers to an idea omitted altogether, the extra expense of the wages paid to the workers hired to hand-sort many different types of recyclables. Because I can't figure out what the pronoun stands for, I immediately conclude that the writer isn't sure either, and so he must know a lot less about recycling than he says he does.

Here's another example with a troublesome "it":

> Female students greatly need a women's health clinic on campus. Such a clinic would provide treatment for venereal diseases as well as contraceptive counseling. The clinic would not increase promiscuity but rather help those who need it.

As soon as the publisher has finished chuckling about those poor female students who need promiscuity, she will undoubtedly hunt for the would-be author's self-addressed, stamped envelope, enclose a rejection note, and mail it off.

The way to prevent such a fate is to reread any sentence you've written that contains an undefined "this" or "it" and rewrite to make the antecedent clear. You may move phrases around to place the pronoun closer to the previously mentioned noun, or you may simply repeat the noun. As a general rule, it is better to repeat a noun than to leave the reader pondering over an ambiguous "it" or "this."

Problem #7: Unsubstantiated Facts

A person can write wonderful, flowing prose and still be a bad writer. How? Just ask Stephen Glass, disgraced journalist and former staff writer for *The New Republic*. He could write like a dream (okay, so I may use a cliché now and then), but his writing wasn't worth anything in the end, because he made up many of his "facts."

The nonfiction writer, to be taken seriously, has to be reliable. He or she has to know how to do solid research, and, more than that, know what types of assertions need to be backed up by research in the first place. Otherwise, your manuscript comes back tagged all over with little yellow Post-it Notes™ from your editor saying, "How do you know?" or "Can you substantiate?" By the time you get the edited manuscript back, you may have lost your original notes or returned your borrowed source books to the library, so you can't document adequately and have no alternative but to do some cutting.

Every good writer needs to have quick access to some basic reference works. We all need a good dictionary, a thesaurus, a volume or two of famous quotations, a current almanac or yearbook, and an all-purpose encyclopedia. The advent of the CD-ROM as standard equipment in computers means that you can have access to the full *Encyclopedia Britannica* within the space of a few small disks.

An enormous amount of research these days may be accomplished on-line. You can get on the Internet and connect to government agencies to verify budgetary information, census statistics, consumer product safety warnings, labor figures, economic reports, and so on. You can track down product information from private companies, membership information and other specialized data from organizations and associations, and virtually anything that's been reported in a newspaper in the past decade or more. With a bit of ingenuity and patience, and a good, speedy search engine, all you have to do is type in the right keywords and search parameters, and the names, dates, places, and other facts you need are at hand. To help you get started, I recommend *The Writer's Internet Handbook* by Timothy Maloy (Allworth Press, 10 East 23rd Street, Suite 210, New York, New York 10010).

I strongly advise any writer of nonfiction to have a fast modem hooked up to his or her computer to speed his or her travels through cyberspace. The treasures to be reaped are well worth the occasional shipwrecks you will undoubtedly suffer as you are learning to sail your way around the world wide web.

An Important Trade Secret for the
Less than Marvelous Prose Stylist

You don't have to be a great, or even a particularly good, writer to be the author of a successful book. If after reading several writer's guides, completing writing exercises, and taking courses, you must concede that your prose is still barely serviceable, then the tip that follows will be your salvation: Find a collaborator or coauthor who can supply the writerly touch you lack. Professional writers' organizations are a reliable source of such talent.

You may find a collaborator to work with you on a flat fee basis, X dollars for the job, or on a speculative basis, a split of the book advance plus a percentage of all future royalties, or on an hourly rate, with or without a share of any royalties to come.

Generally speaking, it is the practice in publishing that the person who comes up with the idea takes at least a fifty percent share of the proceeds. However, a well-established writer with a good set of reviews of previously published books (whether as collaborator or sole author) could make the case for being worth a greater share. Negotiation can be a tricky thing, because it's difficult to calculate the relative worth of two very different skills—professional-quality writing and the creativity of the book's idea person—while at the same time trying to guess what the unsold book might eventually earn.

Another difficult issue that collaborators should be prepared to address is the placement of credit. How should the names appear on the book?

IDEA PERSON
with PROFESSIONAL WRITER

or

IDEA PERSON AND PROFESSIONAL WRITER

or

IDEA PERSON
as told to Professional Writer

There are many other possible variations. This issue can cause a lot of trouble between authors: You may not know just how much anger this business can stir up until you hear from your collaborator who's just seen her name in eight-point type on the proposed book jacket under your name in sixteen-point type.

Harsh experience has taught me that coauthors should always settle any disputes over credits, money splits, and other matters *before* they sign a contract with a publisher. A comprehensive collaboration agreement ideally should be worked out between the authors even before they sit down to write the first page of their book proposal. Otherwise, all too often the pair who worked together so productively on a successful book will end up sniping at each other over who is due what percentage when their first check arrives. Occasionally these battles must be resolved in court, with the possible result that the book's entire earnings end up in the hands of the disputants' lawyers.

Better to spend the money up front to have a lawyer draw up an agreement acceptable to both sides than to spend it afterwards in defense of what you believe is your due. To avoid the expense of a lawyer altogether, you might contact a writers' organization and ask if there is a sample collaboration agreement that you and your co-author could adapt to serve your own needs.

Answers to Writing Problems

Exercise #2: Finding the Point
A. "I won't close the schools to save money, not even for one day. Besides, even if I wanted to, I don't think the law would allow it."
B. "No."
C. "Maybe."

Problem #5: Dangling Modifiers
A. I returned the car that needed a brake job to the dealer.
B. Though it weighs a mere ten ounces, this terrific new tape player is packed with lots of sophisticated features.

CHAPTER THREE

How to Write a Book Proposal

The Basic Ingredients

There are seven essential components to a successful book proposal:

- The Overview
- The Market for the Book
- The Competition for the Book
- The Annotated Table of Contents
- About the Author
- Manuscript Details   33
- Sample Material (or Sample Chapter).

Depending on you and the nature of your idea, you may want to emphasize or omit one or more of these components. However, the typical book proposal will incorporate all of them to some degree.

How long should your proposal be? I won't say "long enough," because that's not a fair answer (though it's a truthful one). I will say that, in general, longer is better—especially if you have no track record in sales of a previously published book. Thirty to forty pages is a good amount for a typical nonfiction book proposal—seventy may be better still. In that space you have ample room to tell the publisher what the book is about, to convince him or her that you are the best person to write the book, and to prove that you *can* write a book. A proposal must make the decision-makers at a publishing company feel confident about investing in your abilities. After all, you are asking for business people to put *their* money where *your* mouth is (metaphorically speaking, that is).

Let me interject here that novels need to be complete before they can be presented to publishers. The same for children's books. While there are exceptions to this rule (for example, for a book from a children's TV star who already commands a loyal following), it is extremely rare for a publisher to offer a contract for a novel or children's book based on an outline, plot summary, sample, or proposal.

At the other extreme, there is the computer guide, which may require very little up front in the way of a written proposal. Many of the successful proposals I've handled for books in this category run a mere eight pages. A few have been as short as two pages. What's amazing is that the finished book is often long (the professional-level programming guide tends to run somewhere in the neighborhood of 400 to 1,000 pages). How do authors get away with this, and how can a publisher accept a book proposal on a highly complex subject— *Porting UNIX to Windows 95,* for example—on the basis of a proposal a half-dozen pages long? They must be crazy!

The answer is, well, no, the publishers aren't crazy, because computer books are inherently low-risk books. Unlike other categories of nonfiction, with computer books publishers have ways to calculate the market with a high degree of accuracy while minimizing their upfront costs, so that they are virtually assured of making at least some money on a book. One example should make things clear. Take a book proposal for a help manual about the newest version of the program called Java. The publisher can get figures on how many Java users there currently are and how many of those users bought a manual about the version that's currently on the market. It's reasonable to assume that most of the people who bought a book about Java 1.5 will need to buy a new one for Java 2.0. As long as the programs keep being upgraded, and as long as the software makers keep charging for tech-support, users of the program will conclude that the latest guide is a "must-have." On top of that is the fact that the publisher does not have to pay the typical computer book writer much of an advance (computer authors usually have day jobs as programmers as their mainstay of income). Little initial cost coupled with a reliable market translates to the publisher's willingness to commit to a book contract without needing a lot of persuasion.

The clincher is that the public's demand for new computer guides has consistently outstripped the ability of most publishers to get new titles into print. When demand runs ahead of supply, the suppliers (that is, the writers) don't have to jump through a lot of hoops to sell their product. That's a basic fact of economic life.

It's very much the opposite story with almost any other category of nonfiction. When it comes to politics, history, cooking, health, self-help, you name it—publishers are inundated with proposals, and far more writers are angling to get their ideas into print than there are publishers able to take them on. The latest memoir about a writer's poor Irish childhood may shoot to the top of the best-seller list and stay there for a long time, but it's because the book has captured the public's fancy—not because anyone *needs* it. On the other hand, without an intelligible guide to the latest Windows upgrade, you may well crash your hard disk—and then you're really sunk. Spending $29.95 to protect thousands of dollars of computer hardware seems only prudent in that case—sort of like buying car insurance.

This is all to explain why the recipient of a MacArthur "genius" grant, a scientist who has dedicated her life to explaining the workings of the genetic code and finding ways to cure inherited diseases—and also a writer of admirable and finely crafted prose—still needs to submit to the publisher a sixty-page outline and three completed sample chapters to get a book deal, while the nineteen-year-old computer geek across the street can email the publisher a page and a half of hastily typed notes about some esoteric piece of software and get an email back with a contract offer by the close of the same business day.

It just goes to prove what our parents were always telling us when we were kids: Life is unfair. But now that we are adults, we know that it's up to us to do what we can to improve the odds for ourselves. So your job as a proposal writer is to marshal every bit of evidence that you can, to show publishers not just that your book will find favor with readers and that it will turn a profit, but that it is actually *needed*, that it provides something readers can't get from any other book.

Each of the seven elements of the full-length book proposal brings evidence to that effect before the publisher in a logical and persuasive form.

The Overview

The first two or three sentences of your proposal should capture a publisher's interest.

The overview is the second thing the publisher reads about your book. (The first is your cover letter or your agent's letter.) It's the overview that tells the publisher—ideally, in short, punchy sentences—what the book is about and entices him or her to read more. Overviews should read like the back jacket copy on books. Try turning over the jacket of almost any recent nonfiction bestseller to get ideas.

As an example, I've picked *Notes from a Small Island* by travel writer Bill Bryson (Avon Books, Bard trade paperback edition). The back jacket begins with an intriguing quotation from the book itself: "Suddenly, in the space of a moment, I realized what it was that I loved about Britain—which is to say, all of it." That is followed by a brief but charming paragraph telling how Bryson came up with the idea for a book about all the endearing quirks of the country he had called home for the last two decades.

The next paragraph touches on what the book contains: "Veering from the ludicrous to the endearing and back again, *Notes from a Small Island* is a delightfully irreverent jaunt around the unparalleled floating nation that has produced zebra crossings, Shakespeare, Twiggie Winkie's Farm, and places with names like Farleigh Wallop and Titsey." That list of strange names does make you want to find out more, doesn't it?

To complete the back jacket copy, there are several quotations of praise taken from favorable newspaper reviews. Of course, the never-published author will not be able to include any blurbs, but there are some substitutes that would accomplish the same end of showing that some trustworthy figure considers the author a good writer. If at all possible, contact some well-known authority in your field and ask him or her to read over your proposal and comment on it. Celebrity endorsements are almost always helpful (although hard to get). Though praise from famous men and women cannot make a bad book idea into a good one, it will certainly be enough to save your proposal from the automatic reject pile—whatever else its flaws. Endorsements by respected or celebrated figures vouch for your credibility and help to assure the publisher that you are not a nobody who happens to be able to type. Publishers must wade through so much dull, meaningless drivel every day that they are always on the alert for signs of exceptional work.

The typical overview is from one to four pages long. Stories and anecdotes can make the overview enjoyable to read. You may tell how you got the idea for the book, how you first encountered the vexing problem that your book is designed to solve, how you came up with that ingenious but simple solution. If your book will be controversial, you should definitely say so. Controversy means that both sides will need the book: the side that agrees with you, and the other side, which must read your book to come up with a retort. Be sure to highlight whatever it is that makes your book different from others in the same category. Look for ways to stir up excitement—as long as you're careful not to go overboard. Exaggeration will work against you in the long run, as disappointment is sure to follow.

During the building boom of the late 1980s there were plenty of books on the market about home remodeling. To get the publisher's attention for my book idea on the subject, I wrote as if sounding the drumbeat for war. Here's a part of the overview from the proposal for

The Home Remodeler's Combat Manual, which HarperCollins accepted and published in 1989:

> Remodeling a home or apartment isn't a job—it's a war.
>
> Each year tens of millions of us add bathrooms, build additions, add fireplaces, enlarge bedrooms, turn driveways into garages, re-roof, re-sod lawns, tile kitchens, replace bathtubs, blow in insulation, finish basements, create pantries, and build houses from scratch.
>
> To make these miracle changes, we must confront an army of workers whose purpose, on paper, is to make our home a more enjoyable place, but who, in reality, are there to do battle with us every step along the way. *In 1988 Americans spent $98 billion on home remodeling.* (The 1989 figure will be **$108 billion**!) That's more than the defense budget of many countries. Some homeowners do the work themselves, but most of them hire contractors or laborers.
>
> There are plenty of books on how to remodel a house or apartment. There's no lack of information about selecting kitchen tiles, sanding floors, shingling roofs, wiring ceiling fans, and so forth.
>
> But no book—until now—addresses the true needs of the home remodeler: How do you defend yourself against the hordes of invaders who come into your home, renovate according to the way *they* think the plan should go (not according to your architectural blueprint that cost $2,000); destroy personal possessions in the process; decide that there's nothing wrong with a hot water pipe emerging from the oak timbers of your living room ceiling; leave foreign objects in the refrigerator; take whatever isn't tied down; treat your telephone like a WATS line; arrive unexpectedly at 6:00 a.m. on Monday, ask you to let them in at the same time on Tuesday but then don't show up until the following Monday; never lock your door; let the dog out to roam;

sand the floor while the room is still wet with paint; ignore the three doormats you conscientiously placed outside and track mud onto the newly laid carpet (which, of course, is white); install whatever parts they happen to have on hand from the previous job; use your house like a tobacco-products test center and consider all open spaces ash trays; listen to their favorite radio stations full blast while you're sleeping; use your bedroom as storage space for bricks, floor boards, and bathroom fixtures; order bathroom supplies that take three months to arrive (and are left on your doorstep the same day the plumber leaves for his three-week vacation); carve deep, lasting scratches in your imported marble countertop; don't speak a word of English; and go bankrupt just as you're prepared to sue?

These people are important; you can't remodel without them. Fortunately, many of these plumbers, electricians, demolishers, and other house specialists understand their jobs well. But, let's be frank: On the whole, remodeling crews aren't known for their artistic sense or delicate touch.

It's you versus the workers. *The Home Remodeler's Combat Manual* offers a fresh perspective and valuable information about home remodeling. The book will talk about architects, contractors, builders, laborers, demolition crews, inspectors, and sobbing spouses with openness and humor. Although home renovation is a serious (and expensive!) subject, unless you manage your home or apartment remodeling with some humor, you'll simply go crazy.

And "crazy" isn't too far from the literal truth. According to one prominent psychologist, remodeling is one of the most stressful things a person can do. Some marriages don't survive the process. The *Los Angeles Times* wasn't exaggerating when it gave this headline to a 1988 article about remodeling: "Altered Estates: Fixing up the House May Wreck the Psyche."

The overview is your first and best chance to grab the editor's attention. How you sum up your book in the overview will likely be the way the editor will sum up your book at the all-important editorial board meeting. (That is where your book idea goes if it makes it past the first one or two readers who find it in the publisher's slush pile.) At that meeting your words, your ideas will be presented to other editors, company executives, and the sales force—and they have to be excited about your book, too. You will be immeasurably aided if anyone in the room has personal experience with the problem your book addresses.

In the example that follows (from the proposal for *How to Be a Successful Fertility Patient,* published by William Morrow and Company), author Peggy Robin uses the overview to dramatize the personal nature of the crisis of infertility:

Connie Chung has it. Geraldo Rivera and his wife C. C. have it. Actress JoBeth Williams has it. Los Angeles Raiders tackle Bob Golic and his wife have it. According to the American Fertility Society, one in six American couples has it. The malady is infertility, and from all the publicity it's getting, you might begin to think it's the new, trendy disease of the nineties. *Time* magazine has run a cover story on it (September 30, 1991); so has *People* (August 20, 1990); newspapers regularly report on advances in treatment; even a fashion magazine like *Mirabella* (July 1991) is reporting on the issue, knowing that many of its readers are watching their biological clocks more closely than next season's hemlines. With so many people talking openly about infertility and with so much media coverage about medical breakthroughs, you might think that the infertile couple would have no trouble finding help to deal with the problem. And yes, to a certain extent that's true. There is no shortage of books by doctors telling couples, "You *can* have a baby." There are plenty of books that describe in clinical detail how the reproductive organs work, what can go wrong, and all the various techniques that doctors have at their disposal to correct problems. Then there are those advertisements and brochures put out by the major infertility treatment centers, all slickly produced literature that soothingly tells the couple, we can take care of you; we can give you the baby you want. (See sample brochure, enclosed.)

It's only after the couple gets into a treatment program that they begin to sense something lacking in all the information coming to them from the mass media, from books, and from health professionals. Everyone is telling the couple, medical science can solve your problem—just put yourself in our hands and let us tell you how. No one is telling the infertile couple what they will eventually come to understand: that infertility treatment, even in the best of circumstances, is an iffy business; that there is no one right way to approach any particular case; that doctors often disagree about what works and what doesn't; and, worst of all, that many treatment centers fudge their statistics to make themselves look more successful than they are; and that in the end, it's up to *the couple themselves* to choose what kind of treatment regimen they are willing to follow, how long to stick with it, and what to do next should the first chosen form of medical intervention fail. These are the crucial, emotion-bending decisions that no infertility guide on the market today addresses squarely. Yet these are the questions most couples have the hardest time grappling with. I know because during the months I spent at my infertility treatment center, these are the things I heard women in the waiting rooms talking about.

These are the questions I will take on in my book *How to Be a Successful Fertility Patient.* Mine will be the first book written entirely from the *patient's* point of view. Other fertility books focus mainly on anatomy and descriptions of procedures. Only a few are written in language a layperson can understand; most are full of poorly explained medical jargon. *How to Be a*

Successful Fertility Patient, unlike the books by doctors, will not attempt to tell readers what's wrong with their organs or get into the mechanics of how the various fertility drugs aid in conception; instead, it will help readers to find doctors or programs they will feel comfortable working with. Once the patient knows what to look for in a doctor or treatment center, what kinds of questions to ask, what to do if the doctor's answers don't seem straightforward—in short, how to be a savvy, consumer-wise patient—then that person stands a much better chance of getting the right treatment, the one that offers the best odds for pregnancy in that person's case. That is the basic premise of *How to Be a Successful Fertility Patient.*

In plain, non-medical English this book will tell you:

- How to tell if you have a fertility problem
- How to talk to your doctor about your infertility
- How to find a specialized treatment program or center with a good track record
- How to make sure your health insurance will cover your treatment
- What tests you need and *what tests you can do without*
- What the different treatment regimens are like
- How each treatment regimen might affect your general health and lifestyle
- How treatment can affect a couple's relationship
- What to do when treatment doesn't bring quick success
- About infertility and the non-traditional patient—the unmarried, the patient with religious restrictions, or in a non-heterosexual relationship
- When to switch doctors or programs or quit altogether
- Alternatives to medical intervention.

Because *How to Be a Successful Fertility Patient* will often be critical of doctors and of the large profit-making infertility treatment centers, it should be a controversial book. Good, caring physicians, however, generally recognize that the more a patient knows about his or her medical condition and treatment options, the more the patient can contribute to the close doctor-patient collaboration that infertility treatment programs nearly always require. The information in this book is designed to help the patient become a fully informed, confident, and equal member of a team working to solve a problem: How to bring a new life into being for a couple who wants a child. This book will emphasize that the ultimate decision-maker on that team is *not the doctor*, but the woman and man who will be the ones to live with the consequences of treatment and raise a child if one is born from it.

How to Be a Successful Fertility Patient is the book for the couple who think of themselves as more than just a collection of tubes and organs with a glitch in the machinery. It's also for the doctor who views his or her patients as people with full lives to lead, not just as numbers to add in to the pregnancy statistics. It's a book for anyone interested in the ethics of the doctor-patient relationship and the movement toward patient's rights and patient empowerment. It's a book that I know will help a great many people now suffering because of their inability to have a child, suffering made far worse by the feeling of bewilderment that comes with the conflicting advice they hear from medical experts and the feeling of helplessness that comes from not knowing how they can keep control over their own reproductive lives.

The Market

"The market" is a shorthand way of saying, "Who will buy this book?" This is probably the most difficult—and important—part of the proposal. "Intelligent book buyers," "sports enthusiasts," "history graduates," "nature lovers," "public libraries," "the kind of people who watch *Nightline*" are not sufficient answers alone.

As precisely as possible, you should name the groups of people who want the kind of information your book will provide. Quantify them by reporting memberships in those groups, associations, or specialized societies they belong to. You may also make use of subscription figures for specialized magazines, sales figures of similar books, enrollment figures for schools or other institutions, census statistics for a particular geographically defined region, or demographics obtained from the government or private polling organizations.

Be sure to name the places where the potential buyers of your book tend to shop. Think of the specialty stores, mail-order catalogs, book clubs, and merchandising organizations that could carry your book. List those stores and outlets by name at which you have contacts or influence. You need to educate the editors who read your proposal, because they are not the experts in your book's field—you are.

Inevitably, when you write about the market, you write about trends—what's popular at the moment. What people are reading, buying, watching, worrying about. Unfortunately, many trends are short-lived—so short, in fact, that by the time your book is published, the trend could well have passed. It's much better to focus your book on an activity that is *becoming* popular, rather than one that's currently in vogue. Be ahead of the trend, not on the crest of a wave that's about to break. If your subject matter threatens to be a passing phase, it's important to broaden your book's focus, to link the trend you're covering to other social phenomena with longer lasting appeal. You need to make the case that your book has backlist potential, meaning that bookstore owners will continue to order it year after year.

New Yorker writer Calvin Trillin once remarked that the shelf-life of a book is somewhere between that of butter and yogurt. As much as they desire bestsellers, publishers want steady sellers, books that will that stay in print a long time. It costs a publisher very little to print second, third, and later editions of a book. The cost of making plates and designing pages is all figured into the book's first print run. After that, it's virtually all gravy. The longer the shelf-life of that gravy, the better the chances the publisher will buy the recipe for it (that is, your book proposal). So in the market section of your proposal, be sure to highlight your book's long-term prospects.

You must also tell what you will do to promote the book. Publishers want to know about your connections and sales strength. If you're affiliated with an organization with tens of thousands of members, and the organization plans to sell the book to its members, say so. Let's say your book is about folk art. Revisit the folk art museums and galleries that were kind enough to let you do research in their libraries and use photographs of their artwork with permission. Ask if their gift shops will carry and help promote the book. Give the publisher every reason to believe that thousands of visitors to those museums and galleries will learn about your book, and that a high percentage of them will want to own it.

If you don't have personal connections to sales outlets, then at least point to the connections that the publisher's sales force will be able to establish. Let the publisher know that there are readers out there hungrily awaiting your book. That's what Peggy Robin did in the market section of her proposal for *How to Be a Successful Fertility Patient,* reprinted here:

"Women trying to conceive will buy anything," says Dr. Melvin Cohen, a professor of obstetrics and gynecology at Northwestern Medical School in Illinois. They and their partners spend over a *billion dollars a year* on medical treatment to correct infertility. That figure doesn't take into account the additional millions spent outside of the doctor's office on items such as ovulation prediction kits, fertility-tracking computer programs ("The Rabbit" available from the Sharper Image and "Bioself" available from the Lifestyle Resources catalog are examples), basal body temperature thermometers, and countless other gadgets, both useful and ridiculous (see two ad samples, enclosed). Nor does the figure include books, one of the first and least expensive purchases a couple is likely to make after realizing they have a fertility problem. As one infertility patient explained, "You do everything you can. You go to the best doctors, you read all the books."

Infertility patients are book buyers for many reasons: because they are hungry for any information that can help them; because a book is a concise, inexpensive way to become informed; and most importantly, because the infertile population is, by and large, a more educated, more book-oriented segment than the population as a whole. This is borne out by a survey of its membership done by the Washington, D.C. chapter of RESOLVE, the national network of support organizations for infertile couples. An astonishing 95 percent of the respondents had college degrees. Close to two-thirds had graduate degrees. The average respondent was a thirty-five-year-old female. Any survey of the book-buying public will tell you that this description is also that of the segment of our population most likely to buy books.

This demographic group is also one of the fastest growing segments of our population. As those born in the boom years of the 1950s to the early 1960s enter their mid to late thirties and early forties, they also enter the years of declining fertility. Yet the desire of couples to have a baby in those years is increasing as never before. According to *Obstetrics and Gynecology Update* (a program for physicians on Lifetime cable television network, April 14, 1991), in the next decade there will be a 60 percent increase in the number of women in the 35-45 age range. But at age 40 only about half of those women will still be fertile. Yet with a continually rising rate of age of first marriage and a consistently high rate of divorce (around 50 percent for the last decade) and remarriage of partners desiring to start "second families," it follows that there will be similar rise in the infertility rate in the next decade.

It also follows that as medical technology leads to new treatments for previously untreatable conditions, more couples who in the past would have accepted their problem stoically are now seeking help. *Time* magazine (September 30, 1991) reports that last year the number of new patients making their first visit to a specialist topped the one million mark.

Since even "low-tech" methods of infertility treatment are expensive (the oral ovulation medication Clomid, for example, costs about $10 *per pill*) and "high-tech" methods such as in vitro fertilization can easily top $10,000 per attempt, the couple seeking treatment must necessarily be, if not affluent, at least middle or upper middle class.

If you're going to invest a relatively large chunk of your income in a medical procedure—especially a somewhat chancy and often painful one—it makes sense to check into it a little first. A simple way to do that is to buy a few books on the subject, and that is exactly what most couples do.

Infertile couples have kept Dr. Sherman Silber's book *How to Get Pregnant* selling at consistently high levels since it was first published in 1981. An updated version, *How to Get Pregnant with the New Technology,* has done well since it came out in March of this year. The nonprofit national association for the infertile, RESOLVE, has been selling *Infertility: A Guide for the Childless Couple,* written by its founder Barbara Eck Manning, since 1977 (an expanded edition was published in 1988). The couple seeking infertility advice can find these and other books in any well-stocked general interest bookstore, but they may also learn about their problem from a wide variety of other sources. The RESOLVE organization sells books, pamphlets, and videos directly to its 20,000 members in 250 chapters in the U.S. and Canada. It also puts out a newsletter reviewing virtually every new publication on infertility.

There are also specialized bookstores that carry only books on health or lifestyle subjects, and infertility generally occupies several shelves. Reiter's bookstore in Washington, D.C., stocks only books on science and medicine, carrying both doctor's texts and general audience books on infertility. "New Age" bookstores also tend to have material on the issue, although usually just those books that question mainstream approaches to diagnosis and cure. As my book will be highly critical of the profit-making industry that has sprung up around the medical advances in infertility treatment and as I strongly advocate a new doctor-patient relationship that maximizes the patient's role in the decision-making process, my book should fit in well with the range of books found in these specialized stores.

Because my book will also address the problem of the gay or lesbian couple who wishes to have a biological child, gay book-stores will be a valuable outlet for sales. No other fertility book offers information for gay couples.

Catalogs are an important source of material for consumers who find ordering by mail or phone a convenient and very private way to receive information on an often touchy subject. The Self-Care catalog not only carries computer programs and special thermometers to help a woman keep track of her fertile days but it also sells videotapes and books. When I called to order the video *Pathways to Parenthood* by Dr. Alan Xenakis, I was told it was so popular that I'd have to wait weeks before a back-ordered copy would be available. Lifestyle Resources, already mentioned as distributor of the "Bioself" computerized fertility chart, is another catalog market for fertility books.

While specialized markets for infertility information are unques-tionably flourishing, you need not to be a member of RESOLVE or on any particular mailing list to find out about new books on the subject. The mass media has done their part to keep a variety of infertility issues in the public spotlight. In September 1991 Geraldo Rivera did a show on "celebrity miracle babies" featuring actresses and their fertility-treatment-conceived children, and spotlighting Dr. Niels Lauerson, Geraldo's own infertility doctor, who has written yet another physician's guide to the subject. Phil Donahue has often wrestled with the moral and legal questions flowing from surrogate motherhood, "host uterus," "donor egg," and other "ARTs" (assisted reproductive technologies); author Dr. Sherman Silber has appeared several times to promote his books. Oprah Winfrey, Sally Jessy Raphael, and Larry King, not to mention the countless regional and local television and radio talk show hosts, have demonstrated their continuing interest in the problem of infertility by the frequency with which it reappears as a topic on their programs. As the number of couples in treatment continues to grow (including, of course, media schedulers and stars themselves), and as medical science continues to develop new methods of inducing conception in couples with reproductive difficulties, the airtime devoted to the topic can be expected to keep pace.

But perhaps more important than any of these means for couples to learn about a new book on infertility is the old-fashioned method of word of mouth. Nearly every form of infertility treatment available today requires the women to spend a lot of time in doctor's waiting rooms. For example, after taking Pergonal, one of the most widely prescribed fertility drugs, a woman will report to her doctor's office for an ovarian sonogram and a blood test every morning for nearly two weeks out of every month she's in treatment. What do the women in these doctors' offices do as they sit around waiting for their turn under the ultrasound machine? They talk to each other. About their hopes for children, about the miscarriages and ectopic pregnancies they've suffered, about their experience with the doctor or with previous doctors, and very frequently, about the books they've read.

Not only did I buy books recommended to me by other patients I met while in treatment, but after I told my doctor about a particular drug combination I had read about in a book, he agreed to let me try it, and the next cycle I became pregnant on those drugs. But perhaps the best example of the efficacy of waiting-room word of mouth in spurring sales of books to women is the case of *What to Expect When You're Expecting.* As reported by Daisy Maryles in the *Publishers Weekly* article "Hidden Super-sellers" (May 25, 1990), "Word-of-mouth builds strongly when pregnant women meet in classes and waiting rooms," thereby helping to account for the million-plus copies that have sold since Workman first published the book in 1984. Though originally rejected by eleven publishers (who generally felt that there were enough pregnancy guides on the market and that only a book by a certified M.D. would sell), *What to Expect...* has proved beyond any doubt that women want to hear from other women who have been through an experience and can tell matter-of-factly just what is involved. My book aims to do for infertility treatment what authors Arlene Eisenberg, Heidi Murkoff, and Sandee Hathaway have done for pregnancy.

To track down the facts and figures on interest groups and sales outlets to list in the market section of your book proposal you may have to do more research than you need to do for the book itself, but a well documented research section will be worth the extra time and effort you put into it. The proof that there's a hot market out there for your book can easily make the difference between "Yes, it looks like just the thing for us!" and "Sorry, but it just doesn't suit our list at this time."

The Competition
This section answers the question, "Why is this book better than other similar books?" Notice that it assumes that there *are* competitive books, because there always are. You might think that your unauthorized

biography of Walter Cronkite doesn't have any competition because you didn't find any other titles listed in *Books in Print,* but that isn't the way the publisher looks at the issue. Any book about a major television reporter could be considered competition. Even books about the news media in general would be considered competition for a Cronkite biography. The test for competition is not whether your book is unique, but whether somebody might buy another book instead of yours.

Consider all books currently in print that are published by major publishing houses. When you talk about the competition, you can exclude out-of-print books and those published by small or niche publishers.

Gather your list of competitive books from visits to bookstores, *Books in Print,* back issues of *Publishers Weekly* and *Library Journal,* the public library's search engine or card catalog, advertisements for books in specialized magazines and newsletters, and conversations with experts in the field you're writing about. Missing a major book signals the editor that you don't really know the market as well as you pretend to do.

For each book you mention, you should say who wrote the book, who published it, the year published, sales figures (if you know them), price, and whether it was hardcover or softcover. For those books most closely related to yours, describe how your book is different— more comprehensive, more informative, making an opposite argument, better written, more appealing to a particular age group or demographic class, more authoritative. You have to persuade the publisher that your book will draw an audience that the others have left out.

Here's a sample competition section from my proposal for *The Expert's Guide to Backyard Birdfeeding,* which was bought by Crown Publishers:

Although not yet as popular a topic as losing weight, books about birds are not lacking on the bookstore shelves in today's market. However, there's no book that gives much information about the devices used in birdfeeding. No birdfeeding book talks about one of the most enjoyable aspects of birdfeeding—the equipment.

The focus of most backyard birding books is on attracting birds to your yard. They describe "how to build a birdhouse," "characteristics of backyard birds," "how to keep cats, squirrels, and other pests away," and "how to plant flowers to attract birds." And the bird book market is large enough to support over a dozen books in print about essentially these same topics.

Let's look at some of the more popular birding books to see how they differ from *The Expert's Guide to Backyard Birdfeeding:*

One of the longest-lived is Thomas P. McElroy's *The New Handbook of Attracting Birds* ($9.95) first published by W. W. Norton in 1950. This 258-page paperback contains line drawings and other illustrations. It offers little information about the kind of feeders, seeds, anti-squirrel apparatuses, and other devices that birders buy. The chapter titles accurately sum up its contents: "Birds in our Environment," "Ways of Attracting Birds," "Feeding Songbirds," "Attracting with Water," "Helping Birds at Nesting Time," "Care of Young and Wounded Birds," "Birds and the Law," and so forth. As far as birding books go, *Attracting Birds* is not very exciting.

Ortho's *How to Attract Birds* ($6.95) is an oversized, 95-page paperback. Although a slender guide, this book, first published in 1983, is still a phenomenal seller. The book is divided into seven sections: The first three talk about birds in general and how to attract birds to your garden; next come chapters on providing specific aids to birds, such as food, water, and nesting material. Finally, there's a "Gallery of Birds," that describes the behavior of several dozen birds. *How to Attract Birds* talks about how to build your own birdbaths, feeders, and houses and what to look for in a store-bought model, but it doesn't describe any particular products on the market. The only products described in any detail are various types of birdseed.

America's Favorite Backyard Birds by Kit and George Harrison (Simon and Schuster, 1983, $16.95, hardcover) also suffers from the same deficiency. There are ten chapters on different birds, but only one chapter about bird nesting preferences. There's little specific product information.

Donald and Lillian Stokes's *The Bird Feeder Book* (Little, Brown and Company, 1987, $8.95, oversized paperback) does discuss differences among feeders, but most of its 86 pages are devoted to describing various birds. The information it does provide is devoid of the rich detail that birders would like. Here's an example of something that's not too interesting:

> **Tube Feeder.** [photograph] Advantages: Is easy to fill; has metal-reinforced perches and holes that are squirrel-resistant; displays seed clearly to birds; large models hold lots of seed; allows options of attaching a tray underneath to catch scattered seed and/or dome-like squirrel baffle above. Examples shown are Droll Yankees, Inc. models A-6 and B-7.

Dedicated bird feeders want a lot more than this.

The Bird Watcher's Diary by Edgar Reilly and Gorton Carruth (HarperCollins, 1987, $12.95, cloth) takes a different tack. This is a 218-page diary-type book that lets readers fill in information about birds they see and feed. Besides containing plenty of blank pages, *The Bird Watcher's Diary* is filled with tidbits about bird behavior, how to attract birds, and descriptions of the feathered world. It has some information about birdseeds and birdfeeders, but this information is sketchy. *The Bird Watcher's Diary* has illustrations on every page.

Outwitting Squirrels: 101 Cunning Stratagems to Reduce Dra-matically the Egregious Misappropriation of Seed from Your Birdfeeder by Squirrels by Bill Adler, Jr. (Chicago Review Press, 1988, paperback, $8.95), looks at birdfeeding from the perspective of defending feeders from squirrels. (The book sold 40,000 copies in its first two years.) Just about every birder who hears about *Outwitting Squirrels* says, "I want that book!"

Outwitting Squirrels differs from *The Expert's Guide to Backyard Birdfeeding* in several ways, the most important of which is that *Outwitting Squirrels* is a humor book, something *The Expert's Guide to Backyard Birdfeeding* is not. While *Outwitting Squirrels* describes and rates some bird products, it's far from comprehensive. *Outwitting Squirrels* quickly glosses over seeds, birdbaths, birdhouses, and other birding paraphernalia. Its focus is on thwarting squirrels, its tone light and funny. Most of *Outwitting Squirrels* is devoted to telling squirrel stories and discussing anti-squirrel tactics.

Only *The Expert's Guide* answers questions like these: "What's the best seed for attracting juncos?" "What's the tallest anti-squirrel pole on the market?" "Where can I find a super-large-capacity feeder that doesn't have to be filled every few days?" "What feeder has holes that will allow tufted titmice in, but not doves?" "I hate cleaning birdhouses—which is easiest to maintain?" and "What's the difference between black-striped sunflower seed and oil sunflower seed?"

To underscore how important your proposal's section on the competition is, think of it as you would think of a proposal to raise capital for a new business venture. Investors (in this case, publishers) want to be reasonably sure that the market isn't already saturated with the product (that is, other books on the same topic as yours). You are asking a publishing company to advance you a lot of money (you hope!), and the executives at that company will want as much assurance as they can get that their money is wisely invested. Publishers are generally not big gamblers. They prefer to minimize the risk. So you will go to any lengths to establish the fact that by taking on your book, a publisher is entering into a fertile market, or, at the very least, one that has yet to be fully explored.

The Annotated Table of Contents

What's going to be in the book anyway? One of the most frequently cited reasons for rejecting a proposal is "This really should be a magazine article." The annotated table of contents tells a publisher that you can fill at least several hundred manuscript pages with fresh, interesting material on your subject.

An annotated table of contents is more than a mere listing of chapter titles. Following each proposed chapter title you provide a paragraph, or even a page or two, telling what the chapter will cover. The purpose is two-fold: first, you demonstrate that you have thought out the book in a logical chapter order; second, you show that there is enough information to flesh out each chapter and make for a bona fide book. Consider the annotated table of contents as a mini-overview of each chapter, describing it from beginning to end.

Here's a sample annotated table of contents taken from my proposal for *The Student's Memory Book,* published by Doubleday, 1988.

Introduction

Intelligence isn't measured by how much raw data—dates, equations, formulas, arcane terminology—you have at your command; knowledge is more subtle and important than knowing mere details. However, facts impress instructors, and facts are the measure of how you perform in a particular course. Most exams don't test your reasoning ability; instead they quiz how much information about a subject you have retained. *Good grades are directly related to good memory.*

Imagine, for a moment, that you had never taken an art history course, never sat through the endless slide shows that explained how artists created their works and why these creations were important. Pretend instead that you had simply memorized the names of the most significant artists, their works, when they lived and where. Even without paying attention to what the meaning of all that information is, you would undoubtedly receive a high mark on an art history quiz. In fact, you could probably write an art history paper fairly quickly, because you wouldn't need to refer continually to the text for details. The same is true for nearly every other course of schoolwork.

Learning to use the memory techniques from *The Student's Memory Book* is more **fun** than learning the regular way. Unfortunately, you can't learn these techniques in school; most teachers aren't familiar with even the simplest of memory skills. Teachers often believe that knowledge can only be gained through hard work, suffering, and sacrifice—as if enjoyment would negate the learning process. Although they may be expert in their subjects, most instructors don't know how the brain works and how we remember information. Because *The Student's Memory Book* teaches students how to make use of the brain's built-in patterning abilities, the techniques will work when applied to any subject.

Chapter 1: How the Brain Works

Why we forget and how we remember: We never really forget. What is called "forgetting" is actually not remembering in the first place. Information that is remembered properly is stored in an accessible way, so that it may be recalled at any time.

Chapter 2: The First Two Memory Principles: Surprise Seeing and the Odd Link

The key to remembering is to *make* something memorable. We remember most easily those things that are significant in some way, that are either bizarre, cause us happiness, pain, or embarrassment, or are just wonderful—but always in some way surprising. The technique that makes use of our memory for surprise is called **surprise seeing.** Generally, those experiences that have a *visual* component to them form the strongest memories.

Creating a frame of reference, something to link the information to, is the second technique for retention of memory. Our brains use their own sort of mnemonic filing system to keep track of information. By linking what we want to remember with something we already know, we are able to recall the information as if by finding the right file drawer and opening to the right folder. And, of course, the more bizarre the linked element is, the easier it is to pick it out of the brain's file cabinet and recall it. This second technique is called the **odd link.**

Chapter 3: The Third Technique: Substitution

Substitution involves converting an unmemorable (or unintelligible) concept into something that is easily remembered and fun. For example, let's say you want to remember the Russian word for place, *meyesta* (transliterated). To an English speaker's ears, *meyesta* is an abstract, unintelligible sound. However, the word sounds like "messed up." Visualize your *place* (apartment or house) all messed up. As you create the picture in your head, say to yourself, "place messed up." Now you'll remember that *meyesta* means place.

Chapter 4: Techniques for Remembering Numbers

This chapter teaches a few easy-to-learn techniques that let you remember numbers—including those used in schoolwork, such as physical constants, geometric values, and other scientific and mathematical figures, and those used in daily life, such as street addresses, banking PINs, and locker combinations. These number systems were developed about 100 years ago.

Subsequent chapters apply the techniques of Chapters One through Four to specific school subjects.

Chapter 5: Remembering History

Special section on using Janson's popular *History of Art.*

Chapter 6: Remembering Economics

Special section on using Samuelson's *Economics.*

Chapter 7: Remembering Chemistry

Special section on using Morrison and Boyd's *Organic Chemistry.*

Chapter 8: Remembering Physics

This chapter will show how complex formulas can be quickly learned, even if you don't understand the significance of what you are remembering. Once you have these formulas memorized, it's a simple matter to plug in the data and solve the equation.

Chapter 9: Remembering Biology

Chapter 10: Remembering Geology

Chapter 11: Remembering Psychology

Chapter 12: Remembering Shakespeare and Poetry

Chapter 13: Remembering Foreign Languages

Most first-year language students end the semester with a 1,000-to-1,500-word vocabulary. They struggle (usually in the days before the final) to remember by rote as many words as possible. (The flash card system is the most popular—though the least effective.) However, with the techniques of *The Student's Memory Book,* it's easy and fun to learn 100 new words *a day.*

In less than a month a student can learn all the words he or she will need to know for the entire semester.

Vocabulary lists will be provided for:

A. French

B. Spanish

C. Russian

D. German.

Chapter 14: Remembering Math

Geometry, calculus, linear algebra, trigonometry.

Chapter 15: Adapting These Techniques to Your Specialized Needs

How to develop your own memory techniques to use on the job, while traveling, in hobbies, and in unusual situations. For example, your car has been struck by a hit-and-run driver. Once you have all the memory techniques at your disposal, you'll have no trouble remembering a license plate.

Chapter 16: Last But Not Least, the Most Valuable Skill: Remembering Names and Phone Numbers

About the Author

Why are *you* qualified to write this book? Are you an expert in the area? Have you taught classes in the field? Have you written articles about this topic? These are pluses. But they're not requirements. Anything you can say about your experience in the subject, you should include in the proposal. Have you appeared on television or radio? Do you speak to groups? Publishers like to know this, too. Where you went to college is interesting, but where you went to high school is not (unless, of course, your book is about high school). And nobody cares what your grade point average was.

Make your biography compelling and fun to read. Make it reveal the person behind the book. Give the "About the Author" section flesh and a soul.

Here's a sample "About the Author" from the proposal for *Saving the Neighborhood: You Can Fight Developers and Win!* (John Wiley & Sons, 1990) by Peggy Robin. You'll notice that this example is long; however, it does more than just explain why this author is the best person to write the book, it also subtly interweaves more reasons for publishing this book.

My background is proof that you don't need an advanced degree in architecture or urban planning to succeed in this field. I am a 1975 graduate of the University of California at Berkeley, with a B.A. in Chinese history. One day, about nine years ago, a flyer was shoved under my door telling me about a plan to build 185 townhouses in the woods across the street from my house. Some neighbors had called a meeting to discuss what to do about it, and I went.

At the time I knew next to nothing about zoning and historic preservation. All my previous work in Washington had to do with U.S. foreign policy in Asia. Fortunately, my neighborhood, Cleveland Park, had a number of activists with enough experience to get the group started. I learned from them, and I learned by doing over the course of the three years it took to defeat the development scheme. During that time, I came to see the importance local politics can have on the outcome of such contests. In my city, elected neighborhood commissions are assigned an advisory role with "great weight" in the permit approval process. In 1981 I ran for my district's commission seat and won, in a hotly contested three-way race. In the two subsequent elections, I've been re-elected without opposition, and was chosen chair of the commission by my colleagues for the 1986-1987 term.

(The Cleveland Park-Woodley Park Neighborhood Commission represents about 18,000 people.)

During my term as chair, I involved the commission in dozens of land-use cases dealing with all aspects of neighborhood planning. Along with other citizens' associations, my commission initiated the move to "downzone" (that is, lower the permitted building heights and densities) two of the major uptown corridors in Washington—Connecticut and Wisconsin Avenues—despite unrelenting opposition from the real estate industry. And we won.

Between 1983 and 1985 Washington's city planning agency was charged with the creation of a master plan to guide the course of development in the city until the year 2000. Largely as a result of the efforts of my commission, the land-use policies put forward for my neighborhood and my ward were crafted to protect the village-like atmosphere of the area and sharply curtail new office construction. Elsewhere in D.C., the commercial building boom continues unabated.

After the new land-use plan was enacted into law in 1985, I became involved in the first case of a development project to go to court to test the limits of the law. The controversial office building's site-plan also required the paving of a new access road, to be built through the northern end of a large federal park. When the neighborhood litigants failed to get an injunction to prevent the start of street construction, I was among the protesters who stood in front of the bulldozers in an attempt to save the trees. That action failed, but two years later we won an order from the city planning office for the road to be taken up and the parkland restored. (The criminal case against us generated so much publicity that it's scared off at least two major developers who had been looking nearby for large tracts for their projects.)

Though these and other land-use cases have been the first and greatest claimant on my time, historic preservation has come a close second. I was one of the founders of the Cleveland Park Historical Society, which, only a few years after its creation, accomplished the designation of Cleveland Park as a historic district on the National Register of Historic Places. That society has been in the forefront of the preservation movement today, expanding the boundaries for what can be recognized as historic. Now the contribution of even the most modest buildings from earlier eras may be appreciated by landmark boards, and so they may be preserved and adapted for modern use. Two examples of buildings I worked to save are the "Park & Shop" building, one of the earliest shopping centers in the country, and the Art Deco facade of a small, Depression-era dress-shop.

Because environmental impact usually plays some part in the process, I've found myself learning a good deal about that field as well. A case against the sale of a large, totally wooded island in the Potomac for development as an amusement park provided the most thorough instruction in this aspect of planning. But by far the most unusual of the environment-based cases I've worked on has been the opposition case made out by the U.S. Naval Observatory against a high-rise apartment proposal. Working with the Navy's astronomers, I learned about the ruinous effect of excess "light pollution" on a high-powered telescope and was able to make good use of this fact in my testimony before the zoning board on behalf of the neighborhood. In mid-July the D.C. Zoning Commission ruled three to one in the neighborhood's favor, and the development was killed outright.

Living in Washington, I can't help but see a great many cases that, like the Observatory, involve the federal government as well as the local planning authorities. Understanding the complex interplay between federal, state, and local governments is crucial in a variety of cases outside our nation's capital: in fighting highway, bridge, and tunnel plans, or in dealing with foreign consulates, Veterans Administration hospital plans, Federal prison expansions, and other congressionally funded projects.

A few more credentials to round out my résumé: I was a founding member of the board of Friends of Tregaron, an organization that defeated an overly dense development scheme for the Tregaron estate (a case that was argued on all fronts: sound land-use planning principles, historic preservation, environmental concerns, and impact on the adjacent federal park). Following my work on that case, I was appointed by the mayor to a two-year term (l984-l986) on the panel that oversees the regional Soil and Water Conservation District. During those same years I was also a member of the Executive Committee of the Wisconsin Avenue Corridor Committee, the Washington group whose successful campaign to prevent high-rise office construction along a twelve-block stretch of a major city street was the subject of a *New York Times* article, "Stunting the Growth" (April 12, l987). Last year I was invited to be one of the panelists in a public forum on neighborhood issues put on by the National Trust for Historic Preservation. Next year I will be named a Trustee of the Committee of One Hundred on the Federal City, one of the oldest and most prestigious citizens' planning organizations in the country.

Through active participation in these local and national organizations, I've built up a wealth of contacts with activists and experts from all parts of the U.S. So I'm able to keep up with the latest events in hot spots ranging from Denver (where a downtown historic district has just been declared), to rural Vermont (where an incredibly strong-toothed development law is now being debated), to suburban Orange County, California (where citizens have turned to the ballot box to veto development directly, rather than leave it to their local zoning authorities), to the beach resorts of Long Island, New York (where creative tax abatements have been used to enable land-owners to resist offers from big land speculators).

This network of contacts gives me easy access to top-notch advice. *Saving the Neighborhood* will have the benefit of input from the nation's leading preservation attorney, an environmental lawyer, and several urban planning professors, as well as other successful neighborhood activists.

Though all this expertise is invaluable, for the book to work it must be organized and drafted by someone who can write with both clarity and passion. "Eloquent" was the word used by *Washington Post* architecture critic Benjamin Forgey to describe my brief against the "suicide barrier" on the Duke Ellington Bridge (The *Washington Post,* July 4, 1987). Articles of mine in neighborhood newspapers have been persuasive enough to generate hundreds of letters in support of my positions in cases before the local zoning board. My speeches and lectures before a variety of audiences, from the D.C. City Council to the Wisconsin Avenue Business Association (a *pro*-development group), have all been well received.

The time is right for a book-length treatment of this subject, and I am the person to do it.

An "About the Author" section need not be long. Usually an author can give his or her qualifications in a page or less. Remember, you are not telling your life story—only that small part of your life that is relevant to your authorship of the proposed book. A good example of a brief "About the Author" section comes from Ken Lawrence's proposal for *Accident-Proof Your Life,* published by Thomas Nelson Publishers.

Ken Lawrence has been a journalist and writer for sixteen years and is the author of five nonfiction books and one novel, including

On the Line: The Men of MCI Who Took on AT&T and Won
(Warner Books 1986, paperback 1987) and *Cults That Kill*
(Warner Books, 1988, paperback 1989). His novel *Naked Prey*
was published by Zebra Books in 1991.

He has written for numerous magazines, including *Omni,
Popular Science, Wilderness Magazine, Consumers Digest,
Washingtonian* magazine, *Washington Journalism Review, High
Technology, Science Digest, Woman's World, Popular Electron-
ics,* and *American Bookseller.* His articles have also appeared
in *The Washington Post, The Village Voice,* and *The Christian
Science Monitor.*

He lives in Alexandria, Virginia with his wife and son.

Manuscript Details

This section tells essential information about the book's length, time
needed for writing, and other facts the publisher needs to know before
offering a book contract. Most important, how long will it take to
complete the book? Be honest. Can you do it in three months?
A year? Whatever you say is what will probably appear in your
contract, so don't fudge here. Eight to ten months is a safe amount for
the average length book. Ask for much more time and the publisher
may worry about your slow work pace; promise the completed work
in much less time and the worry will be that you're promising more
than you can deliver—or else you'll do a hasty, sloppy job.

How long will the book be? You can figure this information in
manuscript pages, words, or book pages. An average-sized book runs
about 300 to 500 manuscript pages, or 60,000 to 120,000 words, or
200 to 400 book pages. (That's assuming the average double-spaced
manuscript has about 250 words per page.)

If you plan to include photographs, line drawings, or other art in
the book, say so. If you have specific illustrations in mind, describe
them. Don't go overboard with photos in the book because illustrations, especially in color, are expensive. It will be up to you, in most

cases, to acquire the rights to reproduce the illustrations or photographs, so be sure not to promise any artwork you are not sure you can obtain.

Also answer any legal or copyright questions that may be raised by your proposal. Do you hold the exclusive rights to the life story of the person you're writing about? Let the publisher know. Are you relying on access to letters and documents held in private hands? If so, attach a copy of the correspondence in which you are given exclusive access to the files. Failure to address issues such as these in your proposal could suggest to the publisher that you won't be able to produce the work after all, or that if you do, legal problems could follow.

Sample Material

The proposal elements described so far will give publishers a good sense of what your book is about and how it's organized. Now comes the part that really shows them you can write. Here's where you strut your stuff. Pick the most exciting chapter of your book for the sample material. Go for your most controversial argument, or the most startling piece of information. Choose material that stands alone well (or put the other way around, choose material that doesn't require a long explanatory preface to put it into context). Certain formats make for good sample reading for publishers: For example, if you have a chapter in question-and-answer format, that might be a good one to submit as your sample. Q&As are quick and easy to read, convey new information, and don't require much in the way of setup. In a pop psychology guide, a personality quiz might be an entertaining choice for sample material. Quizzes are fun and can get several of the editors at the publishing house involved in your work. In a serious work of history, go for the material that most clearly and concisely lays out your central thesis (most likely your introduction and first chapter). As the above recommendations suggest, you must take into account the type of book you're proposing (light versus serious, popular versus academic) when selecting your sample.

How much sample material do you need? At least a complete chapter, and in some instances (for example, when an argument is only partially proven by a chapter), a second or third chapter, as well. If your chapters are very short (say, two or three pages each), then you may need to submit four or more. Just be sure that the publisher has enough material to get a good grasp of your writing style and tone. Be especially vigilant about grammatical errors and typos in your sample material. It's the sample that tells the publisher how much editing time your work will require. Editing is expensive, and if it ends up taking longer than expected, it can really throw off the publisher's calendar for the whole year. No matter how well-written the rest of the proposal, it will be rejected if the sample material appears to need heavy editing.

When selecting sample material to include in my proposal for *The Student's Memory Book,* I chose not to present the introduction or any of the early material explaining how memory techniques work—I had already summarized the main concepts in my overview section. Instead I chose the chapter that tells how to memorize the Bill of Rights. Why? Because most editors and publishers studied the Bill of Rights in high school, but they probably didn't retain what they learned. I start off the sample chapter with an anecdote, which is intended to bring them back to the days when they were students themselves—just like the intended buyers of the book. Here is the excerpt from the "Remembering History" chapter of *The Student's Memory Book.*

It could happen like this: It's the day of your American history exam. You're having a casual lunch in the cafeteria with a colleague from class. You are calm and confident because you've got the course's material under your belt. As you bring your tuna sandwich to your mouth, your friend says, "I keep getting the seventh and eighth amendments mixed up. I hope I don't blow it on the test." At that moment you simultaneously swallow half your sandwich and exclaim, "Amendments?! We have to know the Amendments to the Constitution?" "Just the first ten, the Bill of Rights," your friend replies.

"Oh no," you say, looking at your watch. "I didn't know they were going to be on the test." With less than forty-five minutes till the exam, how are you possibly going to learn and remember the Bill of Rights? You hope maybe you'll come down with appendicitis or catch something from the tuna—quickly.

Fortunately, it's possible and practical to memorize the Bill of Rights while eating dessert.

The key to an exceptional memory—to remembering what you want to know—is having fun. The more enjoyable it is to memorize something, the easier it is to remember. I know this sounds counterintuitive: After all, memorization is good for you; and as with most things that are good for you, like medicine, memorizing is supposed to be difficult, tedious, even painful. Well, just as medicines are now advertised as "pleasant tasting" and "easy to swallow," so it is with memorization. A good example of this is the Bill of Rights, the first ten amendments to the U.S. Constitution. In the popular memory course I teach in Washington, there are invariably one or two attorneys in the class. And just as inevitably, none of these lawyers can recite the Bill of Rights. Naturally, they're embarrassed, but after their red faces return to their normal pallor, I tell them it's not their fault or a commentary on the quality of legal education in this country; it's just that despite hearing them over and over again, they had never been taught how to keep the amendments straight in their minds. (I also chide them: the Bill of Rights is our most fundamental guarantee of liberty and so is worth a little extra effort.)

Here's how we memorize the Bill of Rights:

There are many categories of information that come in groups of ten (or less). The Bill of Rights is one; the Ten Commandments another; the Ten Things You Need To Know To Pass This Exam, perhaps the most useful. The reason why we have trouble remembering what we hear is that we have no way of filing information for easy recall. An analogy would be a library. Imagine that there were no Dewey Decimal or Library of Congress shelving system. Finding the book you want would almost be impossible. But with an organizing system, locating a book (if it's there) is a straightforward task. The same holds true for memory: With a simple organizing system, we can remember any amount of information—and recall it instantly.

Each number, 1 through 10, can be represented by a picture. These number-pictures become our filing system. To make the filing system as easy as possible to learn, the pictures that represent these numbers look like the numbers themselves. The number 1 looks like a pen. The number 2 can be seen as a swan. A 3 looks like a bird in flight (turn it sideways, and you'll get it). The 4 is a sailboat. Remembering this filing system becomes like a children's game—simple and fun. Here's the complete list of number pictures:

1	a pen	6	golf club
2	swan	7	cliff
3	bird in flight	8	snowman
4	sailboat	9	lollipop
5	hook	10	bat and ball

It takes about thirty or forty seconds to permanently imprint in your mind the connection of each number with its picture. But once you've got it down, you have created a permanent filing system that can be used for a myriad of purposes. Now let's apply the system to the Bill of Rights.

The First Amendment says that Congress shall make no law restricting freedom of the press, freedom of religion, and freedom of assembly. To remember that these provisions are in the First Amendment, make a picture in your mind linking each of these ideas with a **pen.** Turn the abstract concepts—freedom of the press, religion, and assembly—into a single, concrete image. See pens, plenty of pens assembled together, battling against a crowd of swords in front of a church, synagogue, or mosque. The pens are trying to prevent the swords from entering the church. Make a vivid picture in your mind's eye: See the action, hear the clanging of swords and pens—maybe even the spilling of ink, in place of blood. In this scene, the pen stands for the concept **freedom of press,** and the image of a multitude of pens assembled represents the principle of the **right to assemble.** Finally, because the scene takes place in front of a religious institution, we relate the image to **freedom of religion.**

What we have done is create a single mind-picture incorporating all three abstract concepts of the First Amendment, linked to the central image of the pen, standing in for the number 1. Once conjured up, this bizarre scene will stay etched in your mind, because it makes use of the power memory technique called **surprise seeing.** Pictures are much easier to remember than theoretical legal principles; and those pictures that involve action and color, or surreal events such as turning pens into soldiers are the kind we most easily recall. In other words, the more entertaining the picture, the more memorable. The scenes we've created are linked to the number-picture filing system in a way that makes sense for that particular scene. In the case of the First Amendment, we're lucky because pen represents both the number 1 and the concept of freedom of the press.

Now for the Second Amendment, which says "The right of the people to keep and bear arms, shall not be infringed." Imagine a swan family (the permanent image for the number 2) swimming peacefully along a country lake with machine guns (representing the right to bear arms) slung over their wings. Again, actually visualize the scene in your mind's eye. (One of my students suggested an alternative image: A man machine-gunning the swans as they float along. I prefer the first picture, but if this one is more striking to you, by all means use it.) The surprising sight of swans with machine guns would never exist in the real world; the fantastic nature of the image makes it an especially memorable link between the swan—the 2—and the right to bear arms.

There are two processes involved here. The first is **substituting** an image of something we know or create with our imagination for a concept that we want to remember. The second process involves **linking** this image to the number-picture, our filing system. That's all.

The Third Amendment prohibits quartering troops in private homes during peacetime. (In pre-Revolutionary days this was a vital issue because the Crown, by keeping troops in people's homes, could effectively control the population. It's difficult to rebel when you have a soldier as a roommate.) Picture a soldier flying into a house on top of a giant bird (the number 3). *That* image should do the trick. Later when you try and recall what the Third Amendment says, you'll think of a bird and instantly this image will fly into your head. And if someone asks you, "Which amendment pertains to quartering troops in homes during peacetime?" your mind will conjure a house, a soldier— then you'll see the soldier on a bird. The bird is a three on its side—voilá, the Third Amendment.

The Fourth Amendment to the Constitution protects us from unreasonable searches and seizures. Linking search and seizure to the sailboat (the number 4) takes no time at all: Visualize the crew of a Coast Guard vessel seizing a recreational sailboat. Alternatively, see two children playing with a toy sailboat in a lake; one of them seizes the boat.

Although I'm providing specific scenes (or stories, if you prefer) for each amendment, it's always best if you create your own images. The act of composing your own pictures is a tremendous boost to memorizing the Bill of Rights—or anything else in a numbered list. As your brain focuses on devising a creative image for what you want to learn, it is vigorously involved in the process of memorizing that information. In surprise seeing, *you* should create the surprise.

Using these techniques takes practice, because as adults we're not too good at stretching our imaginations. As adults we're told not to fantasize about serious endeavors; instead we are made to believe that work and play don't mix. We are educated to observe the strictures of seriousness in all matters pertaining to work, even when being solemn makes the job harder. We're told that there's only one right way to do something, and that means memorizing by rote, which as a consequence means not exploring alternative approaches to memorization. To develop memory skills, you must unleash your pent-up imagination, let it become childlike once more, uninhibited, and able to see things as they never could be. A child's imagination is her most potent tool; during the first six years of life, for most children imagination is far more real than the physical world. What children see in their mind's eye they remember clearly, and oftentimes for a very long time. It is this ability we all have within us that gives us the true power of memorization.

After you read about the next six amendments, take a few minutes to develop your own images before looking at the ones I've created. Your memory of the Bill of Rights will be that much stronger.

The Fifth Amendment is among the most important and most complicated. It says that a grand jury indictment is required in capital crimes, no person shall be tried for the same crime twice (put in "double jeopardy"), no one shall be compelled to testify against himself, no one shall be "deprived of life, liberty, or property, without due process of law," and, finally, that private property shall not be taken for public use without just compensation. (This last section explains why states can appropriate property to build highways and other projects.)

All right, here is the memory part: Take the hook, which stands for the number 5. Imagine a grand piano attached to the hook, and sitting on the bench and playing the piano together is an entire **jury**. Next, attached to the same hook are two **Jeopardy** game boards. If you look up, you'll see that the hook is attached to the courtroom stand that witnesses **testify** in. If that part of the scene isn't enough to remind you of the prohibition against testifying against yourself, visualize somebody in that stand testifying in front of a mirror—that will remind you. Next, balance the scales of liberty—a classic symbol of justice—on the hook. Finally, add the notion of just compensation to the scene by putting money on one side of the scale and your house (or maybe a Monopoly house) on the other side. If you've used my image instead of creating your own, go over it a couple times more in your mind—and really see the picture with all of its components in place. There you have all the provisions of the Fifth Amendment before you, dangling on a single hook—the number 5.

The Sixth Amendment guarantees all criminal defendants the right to a speedy and public trial, to trial by an impartial jury in the locality where the crime was committed, to confront the witnesses against them, and to be defended by counsel. This amendment leads to one of my favorite scenes. See a bunch (a gaggle?) of lawyers, dressed crisply in their gray, pin-striped suits, playing golf. (The golf club looks like the number 6— remember?) Suddenly, they put the clubs down and race to a **court** with a basketball hoop, and continue their physical activity (still dressed in suits, naturally). But this basketball court happens to be inside an actual courtroom, and in the jury box are **local** farmers, all dressed identically, wearing the same high school tee-shirt. The jurors are all looking at a woman on the witness stand, also wearing the same tee-shirt. The fact that she is dressed identically to the jurors tells us that she, the accused, is being tried by a local jury of her peers. To bring to mind the right to confront witnesses against you, have the woman stare into the eyes of an eerie, ghostly face that is floating freely in the air; the apparition has one arm that is pointing a finger toward the accused. (An alternative image involves putting **pears**—with noses, eyes, ears, and other facial parts—in the jury box—"pears" sound like "peers;" the substitution of a specific image, pears, for the concept, peers, will remind you that it's a jury of peers. The possible images are as varied as your imagination, so use what works best for you.)

It may feel as if the scenes we have created for some of the amendments are contrived, at the very least, or silly—especially the previous three amendments. But it only seems this way because you've never applied these techniques before. Memory skills are a little like learning multiplication: At first multiplication seemed cumbersome and strange; now, it's a part of your everyday life. As you begin to exercise your imagination more and more to create your memory scenes, these techniques will become a lot quicker and easier to use. The information you retain through application of memory techniques will mean more to you than if you had simply gone over and over the words until you knew them by rote.

Now is a good time to quickly review the first six amendments. If this is the first time you've used memory techniques, give your brain a chance to get used to this new way of learning. Let your mind see the visual connections between the substance of the amendments and the number-pictures once more. Take a minute or two, then continue with the list of ten.

The Seventh Amendment mandates a jury trial for all lawsuits involving twenty dollars or more. Picture a jury in its box, balanced precariously on the edge of a cliff (the image for the number 7); each member of the jury is waving a twenty-dollar bill in his or her hand. If you can't visualize a twenty-dollar bill, then see the jury members with twenty-dollar gold coins in place of eyes, or sitting in pairs with their fingers intertwined—that's twenty fingers per pair.

The Eighth Amendment prohibits cruel and unusual punishment and excessive bail. Picture a snowman (the number 8) strapped in an electric chair, only the chair is constructed not out of metal, but **bales** of hay. Now you'll have no trouble remembering the Eighth Amendment.

The Ninth Amendment to the Constitution says, "The enumeration in the Constitution, of certain rights, shall not be construed to deny or disparage others retained by the people." That is to say, just because a particular right isn't mentioned in the Constitution, doesn't mean it does not exist. Picture a lollipop—the number 9—with arms, swinging a punch with its **right** arm—that's all you need to turn a very abstract concept into a concrete image.

The Tenth Amendment of the Bill of Rights is the "states' rights amendment"— it delegates powers to the states, or to the people, that are not specifically mentioned or prohibited in other parts of the Constitution. To memorize this, link the concept of states rights with a bat and ball (the image of the number 10). By now, creating these images should be almost automatic: See a baseball field, and pay particular attention to the bases. Watch the batter hit the ball—to right field, if you want (because advocacy of states' right is often associated with right-wing politics). Now, instead of the bases, there are "steaks," which sounds close enough to "states"—substitution again. Alternatively, your mind's eye could conjure the picture of a batter hitting the ball toward the **people** in the stands. The next batter up hits the ball so far out that it lands in another **state.** Still another image is to imagine the playing field as an actual map of the United States, and that the game being played involves hitting balls to particular states.

There you have the Bill of Rights. Granted, we traveled an un-usual course to memorize it, and we probably took a little longer to review the information than if you were simply to read the first ten amendments. But that's only because this is the first time you've used these techniques. After a while, these tech-niques will seem as natural as, well...reading and rereading. But there's a tremendous difference between trying to remember the Bill of Rights by rote versus using memory skills: You now know the Bill of Rights forever.

Mechanics

Proposals and manuscripts are always double spaced. Get into the habit of double spacing even your earliest drafts, the ones that never go beyond your desk. Double spacing is easier to reread and mark up, so you'll do a better job of editing yourself and making sure the copy that you do send out is error free.

Number all pages other than the title page. If your word-processing program permits, create a header or footer that automati-cally puts your name and the proposal title in small type next to the page number.

Use standard margins, at least an inch on all sides. If your final product is to be edge-bound, then leave an extra quarter-inch on the left.

Print your work on a high-quality printer, a laser or ink-jet model with good resolution. No editor or publisher these days wants to risk eyestrain caused by trying to read light, dot-matrix printing. (Type-writer copy is acceptable only if you are a perfect typist; handwritten copy is *never* acceptable.) Use white paper only—multipurpose copier paper is okay, but bond is better.

Don't put your address or phone number on the proposal's title page. That information should be on the letterhead of your cover letter. If your proposal is rather lengthy, it's helpful to include a table of contents. Each section should be started on a new page.

Underline or italicize book titles throughout the proposal (be consistent).

Proof-read yet again to catch typos and grammatical errors. If you find one, don't hand-correct it. Even if you have to take apart the entire proposal to remove a page and substitute a new one, it's worth it to have an error-free product.

This isn't the time to skimp on fasteners: Buy alligator clips rather than butterfly clips. For a professional look, you may want to take the proposal to a copy shop and have it comb-bound or glue-bound along the left edge.

And remember: Appearances count.

The Kiss of Death

The following phrases should *never* be used in a book proposal:

"There is no competition for this book."
(Not true. In the publisher's mind, as long as there are other books on the shelves, there is always competition for a book.)

"If this book is successful, a sequel could be written."
(Duh. You don't have to tell them that. You're just reminding them that if it's *not* successful, they'll still have a pushy author on their hands, angling to do a second book.)

"This is a perfect book for Oprah and Rosie."
(Mention Oprah or Rosie only if you know her well enough to call her up yourself and arrange to be on her show. Otherwise, don't push it.)

"The author plans to interview three ex-presidents."
(Have you got commitments from them to sit down with you? If not, it's just so much wind.)

"President Clinton could write the introduction."
(Yeah? So could the tooth fairy—but let's see it in writing.)

"I need at least $50,000 to write the book."
(Did you get that for your last book? If not, it's up to the publisher to say what your work is worth.)

"Alternatively, the book could be written as a humor book."
(If you don't know what sort of book you're writing, how should the publisher know?)

"The book will sell at least 25,000 copies."
(Have you got a buy-back commitment in writing from a purchaser for that number? That's the only time an author should make such a prediction.)

"You, the publisher, can pick the title from among these...."
(What publisher wants to do your work for you? Naming the book is *your* job.)

"This book is a must for The New York Times Book Review.*"*
(Don't say that unless the editor of *The New York Times Book Review* is your best buddy—and even then, your book might not be reviewed.)

"The author can promote the book heavily."
(Where? Do you have guaranteed appearances lined up? Are you going to commit your own funds to publicize the book? If so, give dates and figures, but if you're not prepared to do that, then don't make it sound as if you can.)

"Color photographs will make this book work."
(Nothing is more expensive in publishing than color printing.)

> *"Everybody will want to buy this book—its appeal is universal."*
>
> (That's practically *daring* the publisher to reject your book by saying, "Not to me!")

Now Go—Write the Proposal!

Where to start writing? That depends on you and the way you like to organize your work. You may be the sort who works best from an outline. In that case, lay out the seven elements of the proposal in that form, and flesh out each part in order, starting with the overview and finishing with the sample material. Or you may prefer to concentrate first on the substance of the book itself by starting on the annotated table of contents. Then, once you've set down what goes into your book in what order, you can more easily summarize its contents in the overview, describe its intended audience in the market section, and contrast its merits against those of other, similar books in the competition section of your proposal.

You may want to do all the research for your proposal before you start writing, or do all the writing, leaving blanks for needed information that you will obtain from your subsequent research. Only you know your most successful work style. But don't be too rigid about the way you work: That's all too often a recipe for writer's block. If you find yourself getting stuck, unable to complete the proposal satisfactorily according to your original plan, be willing to try a different approach. Put aside the outline, and let your thoughts flow spontaneously. Or stop trying to hunt down some elusive piece of information and just start writing what you assume to be the case (you can always change the text to conform to the research, if necessary).

My advice is not to worry too much about mistakes, factual or grammatical, in your first draft. Work to create and sustain the overall tone, which should stir up excitement about the book to come. Take care of the details in subsequent drafts—but be sure to reread to check accuracy, eliminate typos, and clean up any awkward phrases.

Once you are as pleased as you think you can be with your proposal, don't send it out. Not yet. Give the proposal to trusted, objective friends and colleagues and to your agent (if you have one) and ask for their comments and questions. You especially want to know what parts are unclear, what material needs to be bolstered, what arguments seem questionable or weak. Don't ask others to do free editing for you. After you have learned where the weak spots are, it's up to you to make it better.

Don't take your readers' criticism personally—even if someone picks apart every word you've written. You don't have to act on every negative comment. But if you can be flexible enough to change your proposal in response to reasoned and constructive criticism, then you will probably be able to work productively with editors at a publishing company, when you get one. On the other hand, if you are the sort of writer who hates to change one word in your proposal, you can look forward to a stormy and painful time working with your publishing company's editor—that is, if your proposal ever gets accepted anywhere.

How to Write a Computer Book Proposal

These are the elements of a computer book proposal:

- Summary, or brief description, of the book
- Manuscript details (an approximate page count and your best estimate of how quickly the book can be completed—speed being essential for computer books)
- Special editorial features: a bulleted list of what makes this book stand out from a publisher's perspective
- List of chapter titles
- One or two sentences about the author
- A very brief (twenty-five words or less) sales pitch for the book
- Key sales and marketing features: four or five bulleted points about the book to help sales representatives get it to its intended audience

- Comparison with the key competition
- Sample material.

As you can see, much less is needed from the author to sell a computer book than any other form of nonfiction. Chapters need not be described in much detail, no long author biography is needed, and extensive market research need not be performed. In most cases, all the publisher really wants is some indication that the author knows the subject matter thoroughly and can produce the book within the requisite time. Because software makers rarely provide adequate manuals with their product, the purchasers of expensive new programs are practically forced to buy expensive guides from book publishers. So you could say that computer books virtually sell themselves. That puts the person who is qualified to write one in the enviable position of not having to work very hard to sell a publisher on the idea for the book.

You don't even have to print the proposal out when you're done. Most publishers of computer manuals are happy to receive your proposal via email.

Here are a few other tips to help you put your computer book proposal into its best shape.

Do a One-page Summary

On the first page of your proposal, you should summarize the information in the full proposal. When the editorial board of the publishing company considers your book, the members will have at a glance all the essential information. The summary should include a one-paragraph description of what the book will cover, a sentence or two about the author, some information (numerical, if possible) about the market and the competition, and end with a few blurbs (similar to typical back-jacket copy) to help pitch the book. The blurbs may be quotes from other computer book authors or experts praising your work, or maybe just a line or two that you have composed yourself, telling what your book will do that no other book does or why the book will be in demand.

Sell Yourself

Your "About the Author" section should make clear your qualifications to write a computer book. What is your position in the computer industry? Have you written about computers before? What is your education? Put in any and all background information that bears on your expertise. Don't take up the publisher's time going into your hobbies or family life—unless, of course, all your hobbies are computer related and your whole family works with you in the programming business.

Enumerate the Market

The publisher already knows that computer users need new computer guides, so get right down to the numbers. For example, if you're writing about a new computer application, do you know how many units of that application were shipped in the last several months? Are there special conferences on this subject? When, where, and how many in attendance? Is there a magazine devoted to the application, and if so, what are the subscriber numbers? Perhaps you can find out how many callers have used tech-support lines so far. Are there long waits until calls are answered? Even a figure like the average waiting time can give a publisher the idea that computer users are eager to get the help and advice your book will provide.

Sample Material

When it comes to computer books, publishers are rarely interested in a writer's style or tone. They want evidence that the writer can give the needed how-to information clearly and accurately—period. Take a look at how other successful computer help books are written. Notice that most make good use of lists, charts, tables, screen pictures, and other graphics. Publishers always like to be able to advertise a work as "user-friendly," so make sure your sample material is presented in a way that is both eye-catching and easy to follow.

CHAPTER FOUR

How to Approach Publishers and Agents

Who Do You Know?[1]

You've probably heard people say cynically that success in publishing is not so much a question of talent as it is a question of "who you know." As with many a widely held notion, there is some truth here—but only some. Knowing key people in publishing certainly *does* help—few would deny that—but connections will take a poor writer only so far. True, publishers will agree to read a work that has found its way to their desk by means of friends or relations, but that doesn't mean that they will go so far as to invest their money to bring the book into print. For that, the book must be good enough for the publisher to believe that the public will pay good money to own it.

Without connections in publishing, on the other hand, even an exceptionally talented writer may have a hard time breaking into print. His or her proposals may sit neglected in the slush piles of various editors' offices for months, perhaps years, before anyone notices. Eventually, a low-level reader at some publishing house will come across the proposal and be sufficiently wowed by the writer's idea and its presentation to alert a junior editor. That editor, if likewise impressed, will pass the proposal along to a higher-level editor, who will in turn put the work before the publishing company's next editorial board meeting. If all those present at the meeting—including

---

[1] Yes, I realize that according to the rules of grammar "whom" is correct—but in this case I'm reporting the question as it's commonly asked, and most people say "who."

the nonliterary staff from the marketing, promotions, and accounting departments—are wildly enthusiastic for the work, then the book can end up commanding a big advance and a huge marketing push, just as would be mounted for the work of an author who's already a literary star. It *can* happen. And it does happen—probably on the order of once or twice out of the 50,000 books published each year.

So it makes sense, *before* sending out a proposal, for an unknown writer to do whatever he or she can to become known to people in the publishing community. There are basically four ways to connect yourself to people in publishing. They are:

1. Look for useful connections within your own social or professional circles.
2. Seek points of entry into the publishing world.
3. Establish connections with others in your own specialized field who are published and can mentor your work.
4. Become an authority in your field, the expert whose opinion is sought by the media, and eventually a publisher will call, asking, "When are you going to write a book?"

I'll discuss all four methods in the listed order.

Discover the Connections You Already Have

Think of all your friends, colleagues, relatives, neighbors: Are any of them published authors? Call them, tell them your book idea. Writers are usually open-minded people (of course, I'm generalizing from my own experience) who tend to be receptive to hearing about a new idea or taking a peek at a new and exciting work. A common perception of writers is that they tend to have large egos (let me generalize further and say that, unfortunately, I've also usually found that to be true). In that case, it doesn't hurt to flatter the writer a little, saying, in effect, how much you admire his or her work, how much you would value some advice.

It's important to approach tentatively, respectfully, so the potential connection doesn't feel you're too insistent and dismiss you as a pest. The better known the author, the more cautious your approach needs to be. (Big-name writers can easily tire of entreaties from the unpublished, especially those phrased more like demands than polite requests.) Start out by discussing the writer's latest book. Talk knowledgeably (yes, that means you actually have to read it). Be appreciative of the writer's talent, but not fawning. Somewhat in passing, and toward the end of the conversation, you may mention that you are working on a book yourself. The writer will ask you, "What's it about?" (If the writer does *not* ask this question, take that as a sign that he or she is bored by the conversation and is trying to put an end to it as quickly as possible. Later, as you do your postmortem on how the conversation went, you can either try to figure out what it is you said or did that failed to engage the writer's interest, or else dismiss the writer as a self-absorbed, pompous ass.)

Be prepared to talk about your book idea just as you would in the opening paragraph of your proposal—in brief, precise, but thought-provoking terms that summarize your main points. Then, if the writer responds with any sort of encouragement, even a nod or a smile, make the next move: Ask if the writer wouldn't mind taking a look at what you've done (but only if the proposal is in shape to be seen by someone with professional standards). Be sure to offer a polite escape: "…if you have the time, of course. I'll understand perfectly if you're too busy." You are much more likely to enlist aid successfully if you're not begging for help or twisting anyone's arm.

Alternatively, you might prefer not to ask so directly for a favor. In that case, you can just confess that you're not sure where to go with your book proposal and are still trying to figure out how to get it in front of a good agent or publisher. Pause for a few beats, and if the writer is a generous soul, the next remark will be something to the effect of: "Well, you might try my agent, whose name is ——," or "I'd be happy to call my editor at —— publishing house and tell her to keep an eye out for a proposal from you." You know you've really found a friend if the writer says, "Well, why don't you let me take a look at your work, and if it's something I think my editor [or agent] would like, I'll pass it along to her."

When a writer gives you a lead to an agent or editor, you have gained that writer's assent to be named in your query letter. Your first line to the contact provided should say, "I am writing to you at the suggestion of [name of the writer], who thought you might be interested in the proposal for [title of your book]." If the writer has been kind enough to offer any words of praise or encouragement or provide a favorable quotation about your work, by all means include it in your cover letter or in the overview section of your book proposal. Just be sure when your book is finally published to include a thank you to that writer in your acknowledgments.

Seek Points of Entry into the Publishing World

People who actually make their living from writing are few and far between. So it may well be that after mentally going through your entire list of friends, family, acquaintances, and colleagues, you can't come up with a single name of a writer you can turn to for some start-up advice. But don't sigh helplessly—expand your circle of friends. Publishing is by no means a closed society. Just the opposite, it's very fluid: People come and go all the time. You just need to be aware of the many different avenues of access to those people. You may try your luck at any, or all, of the suggestions offered under the following five subheadings:

1. Join a professional writers' organization.
I strongly recommend this move to anyone who hopes to make a full-time career out of writing. Writers' organizations provide a broad variety of benefits to writers of all different skill levels; the opportunity to meet publishers, editors, and agents is just part of the package. I belong to a group called Washington Independent Writers (in fact, I was its president from 1987 to 1988), which is one of the largest and most active such organizations. Here is just a partial list of what WIW does:

- sponsors seminars and small group meetings on particular writers' issues and problems

- puts on an annual writer's conference
- gives writing awards
- offers support to writers embroiled in controversy
- arbitrates disputes between writers and publishers
- matches writers with writing assignments and jobs
- publishes a newsletter
- maintains a reference library
- offers work space to some writers
- offers group health insurance.

Writing can be a lonely business, and joining an organization can be a way to find kindred souls. (I know this from personal experience: I met my future wife at a WIW reception.) But not all writers' organizations are equally helpful; some are really little more than amateur creative writing clubs. What you're looking for is a group whose membership is primarily made up of professionals, people who make their living from their writing. When you learn about a writers' organization in your city or region, ask to see a directory of its members. Published books and other credits may be listed under each member's name. If the directory does not provide members' professional credentials, then try looking up names at random in *Books in Print*. If, after twenty or more tries, you haven't hit upon a published author, you can conclude that the organization is mainly made up of "wannabes." Membership in that organization, in that case, is unlikely to bring you any useful connections—though you still may find enough other benefits in belonging to make joining worth your while.

2. Attend Book Expo.
The American Booksellers Association holds Book Expo, its annual convention, usually over the last weekend in April or May or the first weekend in June. Locations vary, with past ones held in Los Angeles, Chicago, Las Vegas, New York, Anaheim, and Washington, D.C. At the Book Expo hundred and hundreds of publishers—big, medium,

and small—display their wares to entice bookstore owners to increase their orders. In many ways it's the typical trade show, but it's more than that, too—it's a great big party for everyone in book publishing, a chance to gossip and trade stories, *schmooze,* get to know the faces behind the telephone voices, and just have fun. And it's just the place to be for a writer who's looking to meet editors and agents. Everyone comes equipped with a stack of business cards to trade, making promises to call the week after the Expo is over. If your book idea is exciting enough and if you can manage to get the attention of some-one from a suitable publishing house, the "call me" line you'll hear as you end your conversation may be quite sincere.

The key is to do your homework before you go. Find out which small to mid-sized publishing companies publish the type of book you are proposing. Go to a bookstore and look for books that deal with the same general subject matter as your book proposal. Look in the acknowledgments of those books to see what editors are thanked by name. You may actually get to meet those editors at the Expo, so go with a good stock of professionally designed business cards, ready to exchange.

Look for the booths or displays of all those publishers your research has led you to believe would be appropriate for your book. Do not, however, hand out your proposals on the spot. That's a big no-no! If you have the name of an editor from a particular company, find out whether that person is attending. You may get to meet the editor right then and there, or be told that the person will be there between certain times. When you meet, be sure to let the editor know you have seen and admired the book (give the title) that he or she edited by (name the writer), and introduce yourself as a writer who is interested in the same subject, quickly adding whatever it is that makes your book different from the one you've just mentioned. Chances are good the editor will show some interest and invite you to tell more about your book idea. Keep in mind, however, that there will be some 50,000 to 60,000 people in attendance, and it may be too crowded at the publisher's booth at any given moment to carry on a normal con-versation. Be prepared to be told hastily, above the din, "Well, thanks for letting me know about your book. Why don't you drop me a note about it next week, after I'm back in my office?" You promise to do just that, but before you walk away, make sure to scribble the title of your proposed book on the back of your business card, so that when the editor is back in her office, she may keep your card on file, and link it with your query letter when it arrives. That way, she'll remember that she actually invited you to query her and will respond personally, rather than pass your query along to a low-level assistant for an automatic "no, thank you" response.

If you attend Book Expo without names of specific editors to attempt to meet, you will still have plenty of opportunities to hook up with publishers. You can simply wander through the booths and displays with an eye out for those publishers whose lists seem compatible with the sort of book you hope to publish. Linger around those displays, and look for someone behind the table to engage in conversation. Start off by admiring the books the company already has in print. Find out the position of the person you are talking to. Don't disdain to talk to someone in marketing or sales. It's becoming standard practice for staff members from departments other than editing to have a large say in what gets published. When you get a chance—without having it sound as if your only reason for coming over was to pitch a book idea—identify yourself as a writer and briefly describe the book proposal you have in the works. Especially if the other person is in marketing, bring up whatever research you have done that indicates the depth of public interest in the subject. Marketing people are especially keen to learn about any ties you have to booksellers, mail-order distributors, or specialized organizations that could sell your book (after all, selling books is what Book Expo is all about). I guarantee that if you are prepared to talk to publishers about specific groups that could be targeted to buy your book, people will want to talk to you. You will be invited to submit your proposal—and it won't end up dumped in the slush pile when it arrives.

Your query letter to all those you met at Book Expo should open with this line: "It was good to meet you at Book Expo last week. Thanks for agreeing to take a look at my proposal [give title and subtitle]." For more information on what to put in your query letter, be sure to read Chapter Five, "About Query Letters."

One important thing to consider: the cost. A ticket is ninety dollars (forty-five dollars if you work for a company or organization that belongs to the American Booksellers Association), and then you also have the costs of a hotel room and the airfare to the destination. You need to ask yourself if you are willing to invest so much money in a one-time opportunity to make contacts. Of course, if you come away with a name who seems likely to buy your book, and you end up with a $25,000 advance, you've made a good gamble. And don't forget, once you do have income from your writing, you can make all documented expenditures connected with your attendance at the convention, including travel, accommodations, and business lunches or dinners, tax-deductible.

But even if Book Expo does not lead immediately to a book contract, you'll still have the connections you've initiated with the publishers, editors, and agents you met who may well view your subsequent efforts more positively than your first proposal. At the very least, you will have learned a lot about how things work in the publishing world, and have had a good time in the process. While making the rounds at Book Expo, you will probably be invited to one or two big, loud parties put on by publishers or distributors, and if nothing else, you'll come away with a ton of free stuff, including tote bags, tee-shirts, pens, bookmarks, mousepads, and review copies of unreleased books. To register for next year's Book Expo, call 800-840-5614.

3. Start a correspondence.

This is a means of making contacts that I haven't tried myself, but I know there have been a few prominent authors who got their start this way (most notably, Lawrence Durrell, whose correspondence with Henry Miller evolved into a friendship and mentor-protégé relationship that launched Durrell's career). Pick an author whose work you deeply admire, someone whose style and subject matter are similar to your own. Write to that author admiringly about his or her latest book. In your letter raise any questions you have or discuss any points in the book that helped stimulate your own ideas, parallel or even contrary to the author's central thesis. Such discussion invites a full letter of response, rather than a hastily scribbled return note thanking you for your thoughts.

Leave out of your initial letter any mention that you are working on a book of your own. If you bring it up too soon, the author will get the impression that you're just looking for a free ride, a professional critique of your work without pay, and the author will think twice about writing back. Wait to see if the author sends back a reply of any length, indicating pleasure at having read what you had to say and interest in your further thoughts. You may wish to hold off until you are sure the correspondence is well established, continuing over the next several months, before you bring up your own plans for a book on a similar theme.

This method has the best chance of succeeding when your book is not too directly competitive with any of the author's own books. You do not want the author to think that you are horning in on the territory that he or she has worked hard to stake out. You want him or her to understand that your book, if published, will help to stimulate public interest (and therefore book purchases) in the overall subject that you each take on from your different perspectives.

After you have finally brought up your own writing ambitions, you can do either of two things: Wait for the author to take the bait, and volunteer to take a look at your work and perhaps pass it along to an agent or editor; or be direct and ask for advice. You can simply ask for a recommendation of someone in publishing to whom you could send your proposal, or bluntly ask whether the author would look your work over and tell you if it's in shape to send out—and, if so, to whom? It would be highly ungracious of someone who has corresponded with you over an extended time to refuse so simple a request. More likely, as your correspondence progresses, the established writer will, without much prodding from you, fall into the role of mentor and guiding hand, and will be not just merely willing to help but positively enthusiastic about taking you on as a protégé.

4. Attend writer's retreats or colonies.

Universities and professional writers' organizations are the most frequent sponsors of these get-togethers between those just starting out and old hands at creating finished books. Usually the retreat or colony is aimed at writers of a particular mode of expression: poetry, the short story, the memoir, the novel, travel writing, biography, or any of the many other literary forms. Sometimes participants in a particular writers' colony write in diverse modes around a common theme, such as the African-American experience, or gay and lesbian issues, or growing up female. Of course, before you sign on, you must thoroughly investigate just what is being taught, by whom, how those teachers are qualified, and what prerequisites must be met (other than forking over several thousands of your hard-earned dollars) for your application to be accepted.

That last caution about the expense cannot be overstressed. When it comes to money, writers' retreats these days are worse than sleep-away camp—and you seldom get s'mores. A few, however, are attended by some of the most respected editors and critics and authors in the business. Yaddo, the colony in Saratoga Springs, New York, has been famous for more than fifty years for bringing out sparkling new talent.

The more prestigious the writers' retreat, the harder it is to get in. You may have to submit a writing sample or a even a completed manuscript that is judged worthy by a screening panel. Some require letters of recommendation from professors or from other authorities in the language arts. Or you must show that your work has been published before (but not self-published). To find out more about writer's colonies and retreats, I recommend a paperback guide by Gail Hellund Bowker called *Artists and Writers Colonies* (Blue Heron Publishing, 24450 NW Hansen Road, Hillsboro, Oregon 97124).

5. The writer's secret weapon: Subscribe to *Publishers Weekly*.

Publishers Weekly is the trade journal of people who make their living from books. It's read nearly universally by publishers, editors, booksellers, book distributors, and agents—and by professional writers who want to stay on the inside track. What can you learn from *PW*?

There are announcements in every issue telling you who's been hired as an editor at which company, who's been promoted, who's been given their own imprint and what types of books they are looking to acquire. There is advance word about mergers of companies; rumors about companies that may be going under (so don't waste your time sending your manuscript *there*); news about record advances paid, film rights sold, and multi-book deals signed and by whom. There are book reviews, there's gossip, and there's a whole lot more.

Even the ads in *PW* can be helpful. Publishers and distributors frequently buy multi-page spreads listing all the new books they're bringing out next season. That tells you at a glance whether your book will fit in with that publisher's list. You won't waste time sending out your proposal to editors who have only to read your book's proposed title to reply, "I'm sorry but it's not for us." By perusing the ads you will also discover many smaller specialty publishers whose books you might not have encountered in your forays to bookstores. Sometimes an ad will give the publisher's full address—or at the very least, the company's web site address or email address, so you'll know where to send your query.

I do not recommend, however, citing *PW* when you use information from the magazine in your query letter to a publisher or an agent. For example, do not begin a letter to an agent this way: "Congratulations upon your appointment as vice president of the Allstar Agency, which I read about in last week's *Publishers Weekly.*" That tells the agent that you read the magazine just to troll for useful contacts— it says nothing about why that particular agent should bother with your work. Better to leave out how you happened upon the agent's name and focus your pitch letter on what it is about your book that makes it marketable and suited to that agent's particular interests.

Make Connections to Others within Your Specialized Field

A quick and effective way to make contacts in the publishing world is through contacts you establish with others in your own field of expertise. Let's say you're an architect, and you have a dynamite idea for a book that will enable ordinary homeowners to create complete, ready-to-use blueprints for additions or other home renovations. But you don't know any agents, editors, or publishers who might read your proposal. You don't want to spend a lot of time attending meetings of some writers' organization, nor do you want to spend the money to travel to Book Expo, nor are you interested in going off to some writers' retreat or spending hours looking for leads in a publishing magazine. The thing you really need to do is find and put to good use the connections that others in your field have already established with members of the publishing community.

One way to do this is to attend architectural conferences, seminars, and conventions. There you will undoubtedly encounter other architects who are also published authors. As long as your own book idea is not a close variant of the work of the architect-author you approach, you should be greeted as a colleague, not a competitor. You both have an interest in promoting the public's enthusiasm for and knowledge of your shared passion, the building arts. The architect-author should have no objection to passing along some helpful names, and perhaps a few useful tips about writing on a technical subject for a lay audience.

Another strategy is to hook yourself up with a writer who has already published books or articles about architecture and propose a collaboration based on your book idea. If the writer agrees, you will, of course, have to cede some creative control over your project to your partner, and work out the split of the book advance and any royalties and other income your completed book may earn. When you find a collaborator who is already represented by a reputable agent, who knows how to create a compelling proposal, and who knows which publishers to approach, then you may find, even with a divided share of the proceeds, you are still better off than you would have been on your own (with a 100 percent share of a proposal that's going nowhere). Then, once you've established a track record as the author of a published work, your subsequent books may be a solo effort.

Collaboration with a professional writer can also be arranged without a royalty split—but only if you are willing to put up some of your own money in advance. You can hire a professional writer to work for a flat fee—say, $600 to do the proposal according to your specifications. Then, if you end up with a book contract based on that proposal, you pay another fixed sum, say $5,000, for the completion of a manuscript in a form acceptable to both you and the publisher. Your name alone goes on the cover of the book as the author, and the professional writer is simply the "ghost," who wins a line or two of "heartfelt thanks" in the book's acknowledgments—usually under the guise of your "research assistant."

This arrangement is most appealing to those who have such confidence in the sales potential of their ideas that they are willing to stake their own money on the project. However, your gamble need go no further than the payment you shell out for work on the proposal. If, for example, the proposal is rejected by the first twenty publishers who see it, and it brings in an offer from the twenty-first for a mere $3,000 advance—that's the end of the road for both of you. You're not about to pay someone $2,000 more than a publisher has judged the book to be worth. On the other hand, if the book pulls in a $35,000 advance, then you've done extremely well. You pay the writer the $5,000 for the completed work, and the rest—including all future royalties—is yours. (Note: If the book should end up on *The New York Times* bestseller list, it's considered courteous for the named author to pay a bonus to the ghostwriter of several thousand dollars, at least. You must also let the ghostwriter take credit within publishing circles for the book's success, so that the next time that writer sells his or her services, it won't be for a mere four-figure flat fee.)

For those with first-rate writing skills, who do not need to engage a professional writer to put their ideas into shape, here is yet another approach: Break into print in your field through publication of your articles in specialized magazines. Forget about your book idea for the time being and concentrate on ideas that would work with a shorter treatment. To stick with the example introduced above, let's say you're an architect who would like to become an architect-writer. Start out by picking up all the different architecture magazines you can find. Study the style, length, and tone of the articles of each. You want to be sure when you're sending your work out that what goes to each magazine is appropriately targeted in style and content (that is to say, your piece on working with adobe brick goes to *Southwestern Design,* and your piece on gingerbread house-trim arrives at *Victorian Architecture,* and not vice versa.) It's helpful, but not strictly necessary (especially with shorter pieces), to query the magazine first to see if the editor would be receptive to reading the proposed piece. In your query or cover letter, you should certainly cite any previously published pieces in the same field, along with a listing of your professional credentials.

For those just starting out, quotations of praise from architecture reviewers or satisfied clients may be offered in lieu of a list of published articles.

Once you have had your work published a few times, you are now a proven writer. A book editor will read your proposal knowing that you are someone whose work has won acceptance from professionals before, and you have been able to work successfully with an editor to create a polished piece. Then when you're ready to start approaching book publishers, by all means, include one or more of your magazine articles as a writing sample in your proposal packet. If the subject of one of your magazine pieces is directly related to your book idea, you may even integrate the magazine piece into your proposal as a sample chapter.

One side benefit to using magazine publishing as a stepping stone to book publishing: The publisher who is considering offering you a book contract will think, "This author has worked successfully with the editor at *Such-and-Such* Magazine"—which means that that editor might be disposed toward publishing an excerpt from that writer's book (always a good promotional tool). That's a powerful incentive for a publisher to buy your book.

Become the Person to Know

One way to succeed in publishing is to make yourself known as *the* person to call about a given subject (I'll call it Controversy A). Turn yourself into a media star, the "talking head" you always see whenever Controversy A is in the spotlight. That way, when a publisher decides the time is right to do a book on Controversy A, the first question that pops up is, "What about [your name]? The one who's always quoted in the news about this? Maybe we can get that expert to do the book on it"—and so the publisher comes to *you.*

Let me tell you a story of how a person rose to publishing success in just that way. My father, Bill Adler, Sr., who runs a literary agency in New York that's affiliated with mine, was on a business trip to Seattle, and one morning he happened to turn on the TV in his hotel room and catch a cooking show featuring a local chef named Jeff Smith. My father was instantly captivated by the chef's folksy manner and his simple, easy-to-follow cooking style. When he mentioned the TV chef's name to others he met who lived in Seattle, they all said, "Oh yes, he's terrific!" It was clear that Jeff Smith was a local treasure, the star of a cooking show that even non-cooks loved to watch. It also happened that my father knew that William Morrow and Company, a large New York publisher, had the idea of doing a general interest cookbook, nothing fancy—with the sort of recipes that even the least experienced kitchen hand wouldn't be afraid to try.

That was just what Jeff Smith was known for in the Pacific Northwest. The only thing that had to be done was to get the local TV chef together with the New York publisher, and *The Frugal Gourmet* was born. Jeff Smith became the biggest-selling author of a cookbook series in publishing history.

I can't promise that if you become a star in your own field you will end up with a multimillion-dollar book deal, too, but you should definitely be able to get some kind of publishing contract. In the case of a client of mine, Warren Faidley, make that *two* contracts. Warren is a veteran storm chaser, the sort of character portrayed in the movie *Twister.* His main passion in life is finding and photographing tornadoes, not sitting at a keyboard typing books. But when the Weather Channel decided to venture into book publishing, its executives came to Warren with an offer that resulted in the publication of his first book, *Storm Chaser.* That book is now sold through television orders as well as in bookstores. When an editor from the juvenile division of G. P. Putnam's Sons had the idea of doing a children's book about tornadoes, I knew Warren was just the author they were looking for, which brought about his second book contract.

To establish yourself as the expert in your field that the media will seek out whenever there is news concerning your subject of expertise, you must do whatever you can to get your name out there for the media to find. You should do some or all of the activities below:

- Send out **press releases** to TV, radio, and print news organizations announcing your availability as an expert in your field, detailing your credentials, and quoting other established authorities in praise of your insights or your ability to make complex events clear in everyday terms. Your press releases must look professional, read clearly, and be jargon-free, informative but not cluttered—and you may want to hire a public relations consultant to help you achieve these goals.

- Create a **web site** featuring yourself and your area of expertise. An increasingly common way for journalists to find an expert to quote on a given topic is to type some keywords about that topic into a search engine and wait for helpful web site addresses to appear. You may need a professional web site designer to help you achieve maximum accessibility for your site, making it easily navigable and informative for those who arrive there. Be sure to post your photograph (the most appealing shot you have) along with the best (and perhaps most controversial) examples of your work. Quick access is essential, so make sure there's a button the web site visitor can click to send you email, and, of course, include your mailing address and telephone numbers.

- Participate in **panel discussions, debates, and other public forums** put on by organizations dealing with issues in your field of expertise. Your active membership in these organizations should lead to requests for you appear as a panelist or presenter.

- Get signed up with a **speakers' bureau or speakers' agent.** Although you may not yet be famous enough to command a high speaking fee, you could strike a deal with the agency by agreeing to give lectures for a modest fee, the majority or entirety of which the agent will be allowed to keep. You give lectures primarily to increase your public profile; the agent finds engagements for you because there's more profit in it for him or her. Another strategy is to offer yourself as a lecturer to specific organizations or institutions for free, or for a fee that you direct to be donated to charity. It doesn't matter how much you're paid (or whether you're paid at all), so long as you can list on your résumé that you have lectured X-many times before X-many different audiences.

- **Question the conventional wisdom** in your field. Don't set out to be controversial just to get attention, but if you happen to find yourself staking out a minority territory, well, make the most of it. The media generally feel obliged to present both sides of any debate and often must struggle to find someone to represent an unpopular viewpoint. Some news producers like outrageousness—they think it means higher ratings, so don't suppress your wilder side (if you genuinely have one, that is).

- Enter **competitions** for professionals in your field. If you have a wonderful idea for a book for parents about how to bring out the musical gift in their children, you may have a hard time finding a publisher to read your proposal, no matter how engaging your query. But mention that you won the Tchaikovsky Piano Competition in Moscow at the age of sixteen, and you can bet that most publishers will be intrigued.

- Make **brochures and/or videotapes** showcasing yourself and what you have to say as an authority on your subject. If your expertise is in product development or if you have a particular invention to promote, you may also want to buy **ads or use direct mail** to increase public awareness of your ideas while you sell your product.

Don't forget, when assembling the materials for your book proposal to send to publishers, to include videotapes of yourself on the news, addressing a lecture audience, or participating in a debate or public forum. Also include relevant press clippings and news articles in which you are quoted, or brochures, ads, or other printed material, as evidence that you are media-savvy and have documented experience putting your ideas across to the public at large.

The Catch-22 of Publishing—and How I Got around It

As with many things, there's a Catch-22 for writers: To be published, you have to be published. As I've said in the preceding sections, if you've never had your name in print before, you could well have trouble even getting your work read by someone in publishing.

My agency, Adler & Robin Books, receives more than 5,000 submissions a year. That's more than a dozen a day—and I think that's probably a typical number for any agency with a listing in *Literary Marketplace.* If the slush pile hasn't been tended to for a while, say for a week, then the number of unread submissions can really mount up. So I'll make a little confession: When things get out of hand, we just throw out piles of stuff, unread. We open, we glance, we see if the writer has any credentials. If the answer is no, then it's bye-bye proposal. It sounds cruel, I know, but it's necessary, or else we'd drown in a sea of paper.

But don't think I'm insensitive. I'm a writer myself, as much as I'm a literary agent, and I was once young and unpublished, too. I know a lot of what I sent out in my early years headed straight for the bottom of some swamped editor's circular file. And the stuff was good! I'd worked hard on it. It was maddening, but I didn't give up. I just knew I had to apply my ingenuity, and I could outwit this puzzle of how to break into print. (This was years before I came up with the idea of writing a whole series of books around the theme of outwitting life's problems, but already I was aware that for each of life's road-blocks, there must be an effective detour somewhere.)

I just needed to find the right place to start. Where would my writing be welcomed as something new and different? Who would publish me when nobody had done so before? Those are the questions I asked myself nearly twenty years ago, when I decided to make writing my profession. I wanted to write magazine articles and books, but I knew that sending material off to Simon & Schuster or *Esquire* would just be a waste of paper and postage.

So I wrote for *American Drycleaner* magazine—the official publication of the drycleaning industry. Before you laugh—or maybe after you've stopped laughing—consider the pluses from my perspective. First, as I discovered, *American Drycleaner* paid pretty well: $400 (in the early 1980s) for a 2,000-word article. They also paid me $25 a photo. Not bad.

But there were at least two other reasons I wanted to write for *American Drycleaner.* First, I would be published. Even if *American Drycleaner* wasn't all that well known in publishing circles, I would have a clip to show. No matter how obscure, being published in *American Drycleaner* was better than nothing.

The second reason was that I thought, "If I can write for *American Drycleaner,* I can write for anyone." What did I know about drycleaning, really, except that if you forgot your ticket, it took longer for them to find your clothes. So I dreamed up an idea, which was an article about three drycleaners on the same city block who didn't seem to try to compete against one another. How did all three of them manage to stay in business and build a customer base? That was the question that I pitched to *American Drycleaner*'s editor. The editor accepted my idea, and I was off and running, pen in hand, to interview the owners of these drycleaning stores. They were thrilled to be interviewed for *American Drycleaner,* since it was the leading publication in their business.

What next? Well, as it turned out, although nobody in the publishing establishment had ever heard of *American Drycleaner,* it was an odd enough place to write for that my clip caught everyone's attention. Who writes for *American Drycleaner*? Some really creative, talented guy, no doubt. And after that I could write for nearly everyone. Not exactly, of course, but *American Drycleaner* was a very good first step.

For my next article, I proposed a piece on the U.S. government's environmental police—the men and women whose job it is to track down polluters. It was published in *Sierra* magazine. I knew enough, even when first starting out, to target the story idea to the magazine where it would most likely be a hit. Notice that I didn't make the mistake of sending another piece on drycleaning to *Sierra.* I point this out, not to say how smart I was, but to note how commonplace this sort of error is. You'd think it would be pretty obvious to writers that they must research the market for their writing just a little—but it's not. My literary agency receives hundreds of poetry submissions a year, for example, although our agency listing clearly states that we don't represent poetry. People who send me poetry regardless are telling me they're not very careful readers, leading me to doubt that they could be very careful writers. So even if I should ever become inclined to branch out into poetry, it's not going to be with one of those careless poets who blindly mail out mass submissions. Their work goes straight in the trash, and I feel little pity for those writers.

Good writers don't want pity, anyway; they want a bit of encouragement and a fair chance to prove themselves capable. What I've learned is that there are editors out there who are willing to go that extra mile—if the writer will just go an extra mile to seek them out. What I'm saying is that there are a lot of publications in the world that, surprisingly enough, are eager to hear from new talent. The specialized presses of trade associations and other institutions provide many such examples; neighborhood newspapers do, too. Even if you aren't paid a fortune, or anything at all, in your early days, just writing and being published is a big step forward. Write and be published and if you're good, you will find your name appearing in lots of other publications. Be persistent. Plenty of successful writers today can tell you stories of months, even years, of receiving only bad news in the mail. We keep ourselves going by recalling how many publishers turned down *Moby Dick* as an improbable and poorly told tale about a very large fish.

CHAPTER FIVE

About Query Letters

The Problem with Query Letters

Pick up any other guide to getting published and you will find the section on query letters long before it appears here. Most authors of writing guides tell you that if you can write a good query letter, that's pretty much it for getting your work read by the right people.

I wish it were so. But the truth is, in today's crowded market, practically every other person has a book idea or an unsold novel in a desk drawer—or worse, a screenplay. And they're not all bad—in fact, a lot of what never gets into print you can bet must be a whole lot better than some of the junk that crowds the bookshelves these days.

The point is, good writing is in itself no guarantee of success. An unpublished but talented novelist once set out to prove it. He took a book called *Steps,* a collection of short stories by author Jerzy Kosinski that had several years earlier won the National Book Award. He retyped the work on plain paper, and he put his own by-line on the manuscript. Next, he typed a cover letter describing the stories and how he had come to write them. He sent the package around to most of the major publishing houses in New York. Not a single one of them wanted to publish the collection. All he got were short negative notes and form letters of rejection. Not a single editor anywhere even *recognized* the collection as the work of the award-winning author. So much for talent always finding a way to the top.

But then this depressing little tale concerns a work of the imagination. Fiction has always been a quirky market—especially literary fiction. Nonfiction is a lot less subjective—and there's more of it published, too. That means if you can come up with a marketable book idea and you're possessed of the competence to translate that idea into a readable proposal, you've at least got a decent shot at getting your book in print one day (or so we nonfiction writers like to believe).

The trick is to get your well-written proposal read, and I've spent all of the last chapter on ideas for expanding your contacts with people in publishing circles who will be able to do just that. But that doesn't mean you *have to* follow any of those recommendations. You may live in an isolated area and have no writers' organization to join, or you may have no accessible points of entry into the publishing world, or you may just be too shy to approach other writers and attempt to build a relationship, or you may not be able to afford to travel to Book Expo or to specialized conventions.

In that case, you'll have to rely on the standard formula of sending out query letters to editors you don't know, asking for their permission to send along your proposal. But don't just select names at random from the latest *Literary Marketplace* listing of editors at publishing houses. You'd stand as good a chance of being sympathetically read if you just left copies of your proposal on the countertops of those coffee shops in Manhattan most often frequented by editors from big publishing houses grabbing a quick bite to eat.

Target Your Letters to the Most Likely Publisher

You'll need to do a little legwork. Get yourself to the library or bookstore and park yourself over a copy of the latest guide to publishers, either *Literary Marketplace* or *Writer's Market.* If you don't want to buy your own copy of these rather pricey reference guides, then bring a notebook and take copious notes. Look for publishers that put out between two and one hundred titles per year. Forget the really big publishers, except for those that also have smaller, specialized imprints.

Look for companies with names that are less familiar to you, or names you've never heard of. At the same time, consider the nature of your own proposal or book idea. Does it fit into a particular niche? Is it about one of the performing arts? About an event in African-American history? Is it a how-to on a craft or hobby? Is it regional? Is it about the military? There are specialized publishers that are actively looking for new titles in each of these areas; in fact, for almost any special interest you can name, you will find a niche publisher.

As you are going through the listings of publishers, you need to read and understand the meaning of the terms used. When the write-up says, "We publish books on Southern themes," you may ask yourself, "How far west can you go and still be 'Southern'? Would that publisher be interested in my book about the dust bowl in Oklahoma?" You'll save yourself time and postage by making a few quick phone calls to get accurate information. The publisher's administrative assistant should be able to answer questions on the nature of the books they are interesting in acquiring.

Don't try to get a niche publisher to expand beyond their usual territory. They've generally learned through hard and expensive experience to stick to the market they know best.

Beyond checking the publishing reference guides, a good way to find suitable publishers is to visit bookstores. Go straight to the section where you think your book would fit in best. Look at the books you find on the shelves. Which ones are most appealing to you? Which look well edited, well designed—the way you'd like your own book to look when it's done? Are any by small to mid-sized presses? Open those books to the front-matter and find the publisher's name and address.

Professional Writer's Secret Tip

Look in the book's acknowledgments to see if the book's editor is thanked by name. Now you have the name of someone at that publishing house to approach with your proposal, someone you know has been involved in your chosen subject before. Be sure to praise the editor's work on that book in your query letter.

Absolutely essential (the importance of this cannot be over-stressed): Get the details right! I can tell you right away what I do with the many letters that come addressed to Mr. Bill *Al*der: Out they go! The same to letters addressed to no one at all: To Whom It May Concern, or Dear Sir or Madam. A person should have gone to the trouble of looking us up in a guide, if only to find out who we are and how we prefer to be addressed.

The most minor mistakes can make a difference between my reading a letter with interest or with the sense that I'm wasting my time. When the query contains a misspelled word or a grammatical mistake, or the letter isn't laid out in the standard format for business correspondence, that tells me the writer hasn't put much thought or care into the preparation of the query. I assume I'm the recipient of a mass mailing, and I conclude that the writer has nothing special to offer, or that there's no special reason why I would be a good match for this writer as an agent. I also assume that the writer's proposal or manuscript (if I bothered to request it, which I never do) would be as error prone as the query that preceded it. If a person can't write a simple business letter, why should I think he or she could write a book?

Some writers believe they need to put something attention-grabbing and bizarre in the first line of a book query to make their letters stand out. Yes, that works—but the type of attention they get from editors is most often this reaction, from one editor talking to another: "You wouldn't *believe* what a weird query letter I got this week!" Editors sometimes try to top each other with stories of the wacko writers they hear from. You never want your query to be the butt of an editor's lunchtime trade banter. I'm sure that was not the sort of attention you had in mind.

In short, a query is a bit like the overview section of your book proposal. You want to get across as quickly and efficiently as possible what the book's about, who you are, why you're proposing it, why the book is important, why it will sell, who will buy it—and all within a single page, or two at the most. It's perfectly fine to use some of the same phrases that appear in your proposal's overview.

Query letter dos and don'ts

- Do get information about publishers and agents from a recent, reliable source, such as the latest edition of a publishing market reference book.
- Do format your letter applying rules used in standard business correspondence (use a business letter writing guide such as *The Complete Idiot's Almanac of Business Letters and Memos,* if you need help).
- Do look up the name of a specific editor.
- Do spell everything right.
- Do proofread *twice.* Ask a friend to proofread, too.
- Do call the publisher's office to double-check spellings, addresses or other details if you think your information may be out of date.
- Do keep your query to one to two pages.
- Do point out anything specific about your subject matter or its treatment that would be of special interest to that particular publisher.

- Don't do untargeted mass mailings of your query to publishers.
- Don't put "Dear Sir or Madam" or "To Whom It May Concern" in the salutation.
- Don't make spelling mistakes—especially not in the editor's name or address.
- Don't address anyone by first name alone (unless you've met them and you have been told specifically, "Call me Bill").
- Don't be cutesy or overly colloquial. Don't start a letter with "Hi!" or sign off with "See ya!"
- Don't call with your book idea. You're a writer, so do what writers do: Write! (a query letter, that is).
- Don't try anything weird just to make your letter stand out.
- Don't ramble—make sure your letter gets right to the point.
- Don't adopt a demanding or whiny tone—publishers will assume you'll be difficult to work with.

You might also take a sentence or two from your market section, one from your competition section, and one from your "About the Author" section. Ideally, your query will be a concise summary of the full proposal.

Remember, too, that a query is a type of request: "Would you be interested in taking a look at a book proposal about…?" So be sure to keep your tone polite—not wheedling or obsequious (after all, you are proud of your work), but not demanding or arrogant, either.

Professional Writer's Secret: Lose the SASE

Every writers' guide you've ever seen before this one has drummed into your head that you *must* include a self-addressed, stamped envelope with every mailing to a publisher. Watch now as I smash the mold: *Rrrrschhhmmmfffft!* (That's the actual sound of an envelope ripping, not a mold breaking—and it's also a mixed metaphor, but let's not get bogged down in technicalities.) Professional writers don't worry about getting their proposals back. We would never dream of sending an editor the same print-out of a proposal that some other editor has already thumbed through and then mailed back to us. We print a new, clean version with every submission. If the proposal is accepted, the editor won't reply by your SASE anyway—he or she will call you. If a publisher likes your style but still has to turn you down, they'll spend the 33¢ for a politely worded letter of rejection. If your work doesn't interest the publisher in the least, then it's true—you probably won't get a reply without an SASE; still, you can be sure that all you would have received in any case is a curtly worded rejection slip. You don't need that to tell you that you struck out with that publisher.

So, instead of writing, "I have enclosed a self-addressed, stamped envelope for your convenience of reply," I suggest you end your query letter this way: "If you should decide you are not interested in this proposal, you need not return it to me."

How Much to Send?

The rule is: The bigger the publisher, the less you should send initially.

You don't send out your completed manuscript, unsolicited, to Random House. In fact, you're probably best advised not send a full book proposal, either. First comes your query letter asking an editor if he or she would be interested in your proposed book, which you briefly describe. Then, assuming you're going to get at least this far, ask about the amount of supporting material you should include when you send the full proposal. The publisher may have a sheet of guidelines for proposal submissions—it's never wrong to ask for them. Find out whether that publisher wants to see a complete book chapter, or several chapters, or if selected sections from a variety of chapters will do. Once you get the editor's letter back telling you what to send and in what form it should be presented, *strictly* conform your submission to the publishing house's requirements. That way, *(a)* when the editor receives your proposal she'll see you've paid attention and were conscientious about working within the guidelines; and *(b)* she'll be expecting your work and will be ready to give it some consideration.

When it comes to small to mid-sized publishers, and especially niche-market publishers, you already know from your research into their publishing lists that they're interested in doing books such as yours, so you can go ahead and submit your query letter with the full proposal attached.

Each of the three sample query letters on pages 116-120 was successful in selling the writer's book. The first is from a pediatrician with a proposal for a book on children's ear infections; the second is from a computer expert who had previous contacts with the publisher; and the third is a query I sent to a publisher for an activity book of things kids and their parents can do together.

Dear Mr. Simons:

Thank you for agreeing to consider *Coping with Ear Infections: What Every Parent Needs to Know*. As I was researching this proposal, I came across some interesting facts:

- Ninety percent of all children get ear infections, making it the second most common childhood ailment, after colds.

- Americans spend $3.5 billion a year, and our children visit doctors more than 24 million times a year, for ear infections.

- Each year 670,000 children have tympanostomy tubes inserted, making this the most common surgical procedure for children.

- The standard recommendation for ear infections is now to wait and watch, but many pediatricians still aggressively treat ear infections with antibiotics—for good reasons, it seems. There is considerable controversy over how best to treat—and diagnose—ear infections.

Parents are worried about ear infections—witness the number of articles about ear infections in parenting magazines. Ear infections are painful, expensive to treat, and involve considerable time on the part of parents.

By way of introduction, I am a practicing pediatrician, and I also have my own web site devoted to common childhood ailments. I am confident that *Coping with Ear Infections: What Every Parent Needs to Know* will find its way into thousands of parents' homes.

I am letting other publishers look at this proposal. I look forward to hearing from you.

Sincerely,

Margaret Parr, M.D.

Enclosure

Dear Ms. Quinn:

Practical Solutions to the Year 2000 Problem is the book all systems administrators and managers need to cope with the problems created when computers were programmed to begin all years with the digits 19—.

The enclosed book proposal is for a mid-level professional's guide that tells how to analyze the Year 2000 problem, locate problems, and figure out solutions. My book offers a five-step process for solving the Year 2000 problem and tells its readers how to find the right vendors and tools to put solutions into effect—all at reasonable expense.

I am currently the lead government programmer at the Pentagon's Software Technology Support Center (STSC). I have spent the last three years at the STSC working as a technical consultant in the areas of software engineering, metrics, and testing.

The Year 2000 problem is expected to cost the United States at least $200 billion. Worldwide, estimates range up to $600 billion. It is a monumental problem, but one that every computer-dependent business and organization *must* address. Money is part of the problem, but so is time. Solutions need to be in place by early 1999.

Because of the structure of the problem, the way computer systems are designed, and human nature, there is still going to be considerable Year 2000 conversion work going on even after the millennium rolls around.

The problem is as complex as it is immense. The Social Security Administration, for example, has 20,000 programs and 30 million lines of code that must be examined, line by line. Much of the code is in Cobol and other mainframe languages. SSA estimates that it will take 300 man-hours to solve their Year 2000 problem.

Part of the time must be spent constructing "firewalls" to ensure that new errors do not corrupt already existing databases.

A Gannett news story summarized the Year 2000 problem this way:

When the clock strikes midnight on Dec. 31, 1999, many corporate computer systems could run into a serious computer glitch, making the dawn of the next millennium an unhappy one unless something is done, according to some experts.

Here's the problem: When the date reaches 01/01/00, many applications will interpret this as the first day of 1900 instead of 2000. All date-sensitive information, from loan repayment schedules to automated factory shipping software, could be thrown into disarray at the end of the century. Credit card holders in January 2000, for example, could be billed for 99 years' worth of interest on the balances they amassed in December 1999.

The Year 2000 problem could cost corporations around the world between $300 billion and $600 billion to fix, according to the Gartner Group in Stamford, Conn. Gartner estimates it will take up to $1.10 per line of code to fix the problem. Most companies' computer systems contain anywhere from 25 million to 100 million lines of code.

I am letting other publishers look at this proposal. If you decide it is not for you, you need not return this copy to me. I look forward to hearing from you.

Sincerely,

Dana Sanders

Enclosure

Dear Ms. Barnett:

Would you be interested in a family activity book that helps busy parents and children get the most out of their time together? I am pleased to present *365 Things to Do with Your Kids before They're Too Old to Enjoy Them* for your consideration.

The idea for this book came to me the other Saturday morning when my oldest daughter, Karen, asked, "Daddy, what are we going to do today?" I had no idea. Should we go to the playground? (No, that's what we always do.) Should we go to the mall? (Shopping is not exactly an enriching activity.) Sit around and play board games? (Not on such a beautiful day.)

Then I thought about all those things that I really *should* do with Karen and her sister, Claire—activities that would be lots of fun, such as teaching them how to ride a bike, watching a parade, flying a kite (or at least having fun trying), going to a farm, or taking a hike along Rock Creek.

There are so many things that children can enjoy only while they're still children. If you don't do these activities with them now—such as running through a sprinkler on a hot summer day, or holding them close during the scary parts of *The Wizard of Oz*—you may never get the chance, because children grow up so fast.

365 Things to Do with Your Kids is about participating in your children's childhood. It is about reliving your own childhood through playing with your kids. And it is about creating shared memories that both you and your children will treasure forever.

Aging baby boomers who long for their youthful days, parents who spend too much time at work and want "quality time" with their kids, divorced parents, stay-at-home parents who need activities to occupy the day—these are some of the people who will snap up *365 Things to Do with Your Kids*. This book has a compelling hook; it is a book that parents will feel they need.

Based on years of experience with parenting books, I am confident that *365 Things to Do with Your Kids Before They're Too Old to Enjoy Them* will be successful.

I am letting other publishers look at this proposal. If you decide it's not for you, it's not necessary to return it to me. I look forward to hearing from you.

Sincerely,

Bill Adler, Jr.

Enclosure

Professional Writer's Secret:
Give Them Something to Remember You by

Sometimes it's worth putting in that little something extra to make your proposal stand apart from the crowd. No, I don't mean a hundred-dollar bill (although, these days, that might not be such a bad idea at some of the more financially precarious publishing firms). I mean some little freebie that ties in with the subject of your book or emphasizes its utility. For example, if you've written a proposal for a book about birdwatching, you might try giving away a sample bird-call whistle with each proposal you send out. Suppose your book is called *Fifty Fun Family Hikes in the Great Smoky Mountains*: You might attach a keyring-sized compass, or a small bag of trail mix. Make clear that the enclosed product is not meant to be sold along with the book as a product tie-in. (Only a few publishers actually package non-book items along with their books—Klutz Press is perhaps the best-known publisher that does.) The item is just a token you've included to get the editor actively engaged in the book's subject—something to make the editor smile, and, at the same time, make your book idea really come to life.

Sending out Your Stuff

First, you have to make it look good before you can send it anywhere. A professional-looking cover letter will be laser or ink-jet printed, single spaced, on your personal letterhead (or your company letterhead, if your professional life is relevant to your book's subject—and your boss does not object). The proposal (as you will recall from Chapter Three) is printed, double spaced, on good-quality paper—white—with at least one-inch margins on all sides.

There are a variety of acceptable ways to hold the proposal pages together. You could use an alligator clip, or three to six staples along the extreme left edge, so that the proposal opens like a book. You could also use a single top staple in the upper left corner. If you've left at least one and one-quarter inches on the left margin, your proposal could be comb-bound or glue-bound at a copying shop, at the cost of a couple of dollars for the binding. For a few more dollars you could have a laminated front and back cover put on. Or you could simply buy a colored pocket folder, label it neatly, and slip the proposal into the inside right pocket.

Whether the pages are clipped or bound together, make sure they are all numbered consecutively throughout the book (not just within chapters). When an editor takes a stack of proposals to the beach over the weekend, and they get knocked over by a carelessly thrown volleyball, it can happen that papers get knocked out of place, and the editor has to reassemble the manuscripts by hand. You don't want to make it impossible to put your accidentally scrambled work back in order.

Now for packaging. Put the cover letter over the proposal but don't staple, clip, or bind the cover letter to the proposal. Slip both inside a flat envelope, facing backwards, so that when the envelope is opened, the cover letter and proposal come out facing the reader.

What kind of envelope? I prefer Tyvek®, an almost indestructible but lightweight material that will repel rain, hail, snow, and the spilled coffee of careless mailroom workers. Other writers favor padded or bubblewrap-lined envelopes. Whichever you choose, the envelope should be large enough for your materials to slip in and out easily, but not so large as to rattle around a lot once inside.

A lengthy proposal may not fit inside a standard flat envelope. If that's the case, then go to an office supply store and buy the right size manuscript box, eight and three-quarters by eleven and a quarter, times the thickness of your proposal (as near to the exact measurement as you can find).

If your printer can handle labels, then print the editor's name and address in a large, clean, easily readable font, and affix the label to the middle of the envelope. If your printer doesn't do labels, then in your cleanest, neatest handwriting, in black or dark blue ink, write the mailing information on the label and stick it on.

First Class U.S. Mail is the normal way publishers receive proposals. Whatever you do, don't let your package arrive with postage due. Either weigh it yourself and stamp it sufficiently, or let the postal clerk do it for you.

Do not send your package by registered or certified mail, return receipt requested. If no one happens to be in the publisher's office when the mail carrier arrives, your package will be brought back to the post office to languish until the publisher sends someone to sign for it. Let me tell you, from the small-business owner's perspective, it's very annoying to have to do that to get your mail. You may think, if you're mailing to a big publisher, that there will always be an employee on hand to receive your package, and so why not assure yourself of delivery by asking for a return receipt? But even with big publishers, there is nothing to be gained. If your package is going to get lost, chances are it will happen somewhere between the company's mailroom and the editor's desk, not between your local mailbox or post office and the publisher's well-known address.

I know that many of our citizens have developed disdain for the U.S. Mail (they call it "snail mail") and so prefer to use an alternative. Regular ground delivery by United Parcel Service (UPS) is a perfectly acceptable way to send a proposal to a publisher. So is Federal Express, UPS Overnight, or one of the other air delivery services— but I don't especially recommend it: It says you're overeager, that you think your proposal needs to be seen as soon as possible.

On the other hand, there are a few specific circumstances in which you will really need to get your proposal to a particular editor in a hurry. Let's say the editor has read your initial query and called you to say, "I love it! But I'm going on vacation this week, and I'd really like to get your book idea before our next editorial board meeting this Thursday, before I leave—can you do that?" Then absolutely, positively send it by overnight express.

Another justification for FedExing a proposal is if your book idea is so topical that it ties perfectly with something that is today's front-page news. Clip the headline, insert it in the package, and get it out before interested editors while "the buzz" is still in the air.

I would never fax in a proposal unless specifically invited to do so—and then only if the proposal is under a certain length, say fewer than ten pages.

I would definitely not email my proposal to an editor—unless it was for a computer book, and all my prior correspondence with that editor had been conducted via email. (An unthinking would-be author once emailed me an extremely long proposal containing many megabytes' worth of photos, and downloading it would have tied up my computer for hours. As it happens, I'm computer-savvy enough to have figured out how to terminate the email attempt, and I sent that author a blistering reprimand for having tried to hijack my computer's attention.)

Nor would I use a messenger service to send a proposal over to an editor's office; nor would I hand-deliver it—even if the editor worked in an office building across the street from mine. Both of these means imply that I expect the editor to drop everything and look at my work right away. Sending by the usual means is the way to show that you understand how publishing works—that it's normally a slow-paced and deliberative sort of process. Authors need to have patience—or at least give the publisher the impression that they have patience and won't be overly anxious while awaiting an editor's response to their work.

Keeping Track of Your Progress

You need a way to keep tabs on where your proposal has been, who's seen it, and how they responded. The simplest way is to keep a logbook. You may do this on your computer, in a spiral notebook, in a file folder, in an index card file, or by any other system you design—as long as it works for you.

Your logbook page may look something like this:

Submission Record for *Fifty Fun Family Hikes in the Great Smoky Mountains*

Type of Submission	Sent to	By	Date	Notes	Response and Date Received	Follow-up
Cover letter with full proposal	Ms. Small Publisher Greentree Books, Inc. 1 Birch Road Quaint Town, CT 00000	U.S. Mail	1/3	Included six sample trail maps.	Called 2/16, asked to see 3 sample chapters.	Promised requested sample chapters by 5/1. ❑ **check when sent**
Query letter and outline	Ms. Well-Known Editor Major Publishing House 1234 5th Avenue Suite 0000 New York, NY 10000	U.S. Mail	1/9		Note rec'd, 2/27, asking to see full proposal.	Full proposal sent 2/28. Awaiting response.
Cover letter with full proposal	Mr. Hotshot Agent Hotshot & Associates 123456 Endless Blvd. Los Angeles, CA 90000	U.S. Mail	2/3	Brother-in-law is current client of this agent; he called and asked if agent could take a look.	No response so far.	Have asked brother-in-law to call Hotshot to see if he's had a chance to look proposal over yet. Says he will when he's back from vacation mid- Apr.

Following Up

How long should you allow a publisher or agent to look at your submission before following up? That depends on several things: *(a)* whether your submission was unsolicited or sent because an editor had responded positively to your initial query letter, *(b)* whether or not you have had personal contact with the editor before, *(c)* which publishing company has your work and how long that company typically takes to get back to writers, and *(d)* your own level of patience (or impatience).

If you've taken my advice to omit the SASE, then you ought to assume when you've had no sign of interest from the publisher after ten weeks that the answer is no. I see nothing to be gained from a follow-up letter under those circumstances. On the other hand, when an editor has enthusiastically requested your book proposal in response to your query letter, then you know you've got a pretty good shot at a "yes," so a follow-up is definitely worthwhile. If you've had personal contact with that editor before (she's called you on the phone, is someone you've met, or is a friend of a friend of yours), then a brief, polite telephone call won't be taken amiss. But if the whole of your contact with the editor has been through the written word, then stick to that. A note that says, in effect, "It's been *X* weeks since I heard from you about my proposal," should be sufficient to let you know what's up.

Before writing or calling, it's always a good idea to know whether the editor is, in fact, slow to respond, or is operating at the normal, deliberate pace of that publishing house. For solicited submissions, check for word about response times in the editor's letter to you, or look over any telephone notes you may have taken when the editor called you in response to your query. (You did take notes, didn't you? And you saved them in a file, right?) For unsolicited submissions made in conformity with a publishing company's submission guidelines, check to see if a standard response time is listed in those guidelines. If you don't have a set of submission guidelines, then a quick telephone call to the company's main number should provide you with the information you seek. On no account should you call and ask for an editor or a company executive to answer your questions about response times.

You might want to allow two or three extra weeks beyond the company's stated response time before you inquire about the status of your submission. It could well be a busy time for the company, or there could have been a snarl-up for some reason and things just happen to be backed up. There is seldom anything to be gained in pressuring a publisher to speed up a response. You never want to give a publisher the impression that you are pushy and difficult to work with.

One method of contact I particularly recommend for routine questions and submission follow-ups is email. An editor can respond at his or her leisure or can direct a lower-level employee to handle the matter. Email is nonintrusive and quick. As most, if not all, publishing companies are wired to the Internet these days, it will be well worth your while to open an email account for yourself, if you don't already have one.

Finding an Agent

Suppose you don't want to do the querying yourself. You feel you're not a good pitchperson for your own work, nor do you have the time to do the research needed to scout out suitable publishers. Then what you need is an agent to do these things for you.

Of course, getting a good agent these days is almost as hard as finding a publisher. It's yet another of the literary world's Catch-22s: You can't get an agent to represent you if you haven't already been published—but you can't get a publisher to take your work seriously unless you have an agent.

Fortunately, in this case, the Catch-22 circle is not completely closed. It's probably true that your unrepresented work won't get the scrutiny it deserves at a major publishing house, but that's usually not the case at the smaller or even mid-sized publishers you approach. In fact, the majority of the books put out by some smaller publishing companies are from writers who submitted their proposals directly, without agents.

Still, an agent can do a lot for a writer besides get the book read by editors who would never deign to read what's in their slush piles. A good agent will try to match the writer with the particular publisher, as well as the particular editor at that publisher, who, in the agent's experience, is best suited to work with that writer's particular talent. A good agent will give you an edge in contract negotiations—which in most publishing deals is well worth the agent's commission. An agent can help to arbitrate problems as the book is being developed—for example, to win you a little extra time to complete the manuscript beyond what your book contract allows. An agent can be a handholder or a shoulder to cry on. He or she can make the difference between a writer who does one so-so book and then never does another one, and the next literary sensation.

So how can you go about getting yourself one of these wizards of the publishing world? As with finding a publisher directly, you look for any personal contacts you might have (or might be able to establish). Check your friends, colleagues, neighbors, business associates, relatives, and anyone else who might be able to recommend a name. If you come up blank that way, then try expanding your circle to get to know people in publishing who could recommend an agent to you (or could recommend your work to an agent).

Then there's always the reference book method of finding agents. You look up agents and agencies in the appropriate section of the latest edition of *Literary Marketplace* or *Writer's Market,* paying close attention to what each write-up says about the sort of work a particular agent handles and how queries and proposals are to be submitted. You may also find it helpful to buy a copy of the paperback guide sponsored by Poets & Writers, Inc. called *Literary Agents: A Writer's Guide* (by Adam Begley, published by Penguin Books).

If the agency specializes in a particular category or form of literary endeavor, be sure your submission fits the bill. Send your material to the attention of the person listed in the reference guide as the contact—with the name, of course, spelled correctly, along with all other details checked for accuracy.

Your query letter to a literary agent will be much the same as your query to a publisher (see sample, page 129). The main difference will be what steps you take when you get a positive response.

When a publisher calls to say that your book proposal has been accepted, you are usually sent a contract in short order, and if you accept its terms, you have a book deal. It's usually fairly straightforward. There aren't a lot of publishers out there who will try to hoodwink you or jerk you around. Legitimate publishers don't ask for money from the writers they want to publish. If they turn out to be fly-by-night, you may never see the check they said was "in the mail"—but at least they don't make *you* pay *them.*

Not so for some agents. There are more than a few hucksters out there who never sell a book to a publisher. The only way they make money is by taking it from naïve and trusting writers. First they ask you for a hefty "reading fee." This is almost always a scam. When agents get paid by writers for reading manuscripts and proposals, there's little incentive for them to spend time trying to sell those works to publishers. Volume is where their real money come from, so they try to increase the number of clients who send in reading fees. My advice is simple: Stay away from these agents!

Also, beware of agents who advertise. It's not necessary for an established, reputable literary agent to go hunting for writers to represent—we're pursued eagerly by writers, more than we can handle. You've got to wonder what's wrong with an agent who needs to drum up business.

Another thing to watch out for is the promise that your book will sell once you've let a "manuscript doctor" fix it up. The agent then asks for your agreement to let an in-agency editor "clean up" the manuscript—at so many dollars per page. Or the agent may recommend that you hire an independent "manuscript doctor" to put your book in shape to be represented—omitting to tell you that the "independent" consultant in fact kicks back a portion of his or her fee to the agent who recommends a paying client. It's very rare, after a writer has already invested thousands of dollars on editing, for the agent to go on to sell the work to a publisher.

You should be prepared to have an agent charge you for the cost of copying, postage, messenger fees, and other incidentals involved in the representation of your work to publishers. There's nothing unethical about this; in fact, the majority of agents do pass along these costs. You just need to know ahead of time what those charges are, make sure they're reasonable (so that, for example, you're not being charged a dollar a page for copying), and understand how they're to be paid. You don't want the agent to come back to you after six months, saying, "Sorry, I couldn't sell your book, and by the way, here's a bill for $300 for the expenses incurred in sending out your work." Some agents will simply deduct charges from the commission they make when and if they sell your work; others bill you regularly—but in either case, you should ask to see an itemization of the money spent on your behalf.

Here is a sample query letter:

Dear Mr. Adler:

Would you be interested in representing my book, *Germ-Proof Your Life*—a book that tells how to protect yourself from germ-caused disease?

Food-borne and other microbial illnesses are on the rise: Most eggs you buy in the grocery store are contaminated with salmonella; antibiotic-resistant tuberculosis is gaining ground; sexually transmitted diseases are turning deadly; rabies and Lyme disease are rampant in many parts of the country. Exotic microbes, once associated entirely with Third World countries, are showing up in major American cities. Germs appear where they never did before: Your municipal water supply may well be contaminated with campylobacter or cryptosporidium, beef and apple cider with deadly *e. coli 0157,* fruits with cyclospora. Each year, many tens of thousands of people become sick because of what they drink or eat; many die. I know about this personally, because six years ago, I became sick with salmonella: After intense abdominal pain, I ended up in the operating room to have four inches of my large intestine removed, because the bacteria had killed it. If this could happen to an athletic thirty-three-year old (I'm a marathoner, long-distance swimmer, and mountain biker), it could happen to anyone—and does.

People are increasingly worried about microbes. *Oprah, Maury Povich, Hard Copy, Dateline NBC, 20-20,* and other shows have recently devoted programs to the problem of food safety. *E. coli* was the cover story of *Time* magazine, August 3, 1998. Whenever there is a major outbreak of food poisoning, it is front page news.

According to a Reuter's news report today:

> The U.S. Centers for Disease Control and Prevention (CDC) said bacteria such as salmonella and E. coli accounted for 79 percent of food-borne disease outbreaks and 90 percent of individual cases between 1988 and 1992.The agency said most cases of food-borne illnesses go unreported. A surveillance system detected an average of 15,475 cases and 14 deaths every year, however, the CDC estimates there are 6 million cases of food-borne illnesses annually.

Books about the Ebola virus and other outbreaks have been very successful. Now, with *Germ-Proof Your Life,* there's a book about the practical steps you can take to protect yourself from these increasingly prevalent diseases.

Germ-Proof Your Life provides consumers with accurate—and practical—information they can use to protect themselves and their children from deadly microbes. Until the government and food industry can make food perfectly safe—something that may never be accomplished—consumers will have to be alert to what they can, and must, do to prevent disease. This is an important book for parents, the elderly, people with HIV, cancer patients, and others with compromised immune systems.

By way of introduction, I am a research biologist, specializing in infectious diseases. I am the author of over a dozen articles for various medical journals, including *The New England Journal of Medicine.*

I look forward to hearing from you.

Sincerely,

William R. Jay

Enclosure

CHAPTER SIX

Top Editors Tell What Makes a Book Proposal Sell

An agent's opinion about publishing is one thing, but editors have their own take on what makes a proposal worth publishing. With that in mind, I interviewed twelve top editors from very different companies, from a large New York firm like William Morrow and Company, to the small and specialized health publisher, People's Medical Society, to find out how proposals are evaluated where they work.

You'll notice certain common themes running through the answers given by the editors, despite the differences in the size and location of their companies. The importance of a polished look, the abhorrence of misspelled names and unsubstantiated assertions, annoyance at improper formatting—these points are made again and again. Yet you'll also find one editor saying something that completely contradicts another's view. This one says the heart of the proposal is the sample chapter, while that one says it's the annotated table of contents, and that she doesn't always bother to read the submitted sample. That's to be expected in a field as subjective as book publishing. The main thing to remember when submitting your work to a publisher is that it's the practice in *that* publishing house that counts. Before you send your work to a particular editor, find out what *that* editor appreciates most in a book proposal, and do your best to make your work live up to—or exceed—those expectations.

Toni Sciarra, William Morrow and Company

How important is market information supplied by author?

Very important. Keep in mind you're helping the editor pitch this project to his or her colleagues and boss. Don't assume the editor knows the statistics or markets. If you were going after a bank loan, wouldn't you give the loan officer every bit of information you think would help secure the necessary money? With a book proposal you are asking for money. And you only get one chance. Market research is also a good way for authors to sharpen the editorial focus of their project, angling it toward the market's interests and needs.

I like to see demographic statistics. Also, it's crucial to analyze the competitive books already published on the subject. This ends up becoming part of the editor's pitch to the sales force at the sales conference—it is what they will in turn use to secure placement in bookstores. Consider competition analysis your chance to speak to booksellers about why they should stock your book, when they've probably got similar titles on their shelves already.

How accurate is that marketing information? Cite the source so it can be checked.

What about sample chapters?

Yes, I like to see a sample chapter. I want to see how well you can write. I want to get some understanding of what kind of editorial work might be needed, which affects not just the content, but also the publishing schedule—no one makes money on a book until it is published. Yes, I do read that sample chapter.

What does a sample chapter tell you?

It tells me how well you write. It tells me that you have the patience to sit down and think through your ideas. (Not everyone who wants to write a book has the patience to do so.) It tells me that you are serious about writing this book, and that I should take it seriously, too. It tells me you have encountered and solved the structural problems that arise in executing a chapter, and that you could conceivably be able to extend this capacity to later chapters as well.

When can an author not include sample chapter?

If there is a strong and very detailed chapter outline, a highly developed competition and marketing analysis, and strong sales success with a previously published book, a sample chapter may not be necessary. When in doubt, however, include it. If you're worried that your writing won't be good enough, bear in mind that if an editor loves the subject and thinks they can help pull the material into shape through editing, they may buy the project anyway. Or they may decline it but offer suggestions for improving the work. Or they may express interest in reevaluating it after you revise it. If your bad writing comes to light once a contract is made (when you deliver your partial or complete manuscript to your editor), you run the risk of the contract being canceled because the manuscript is unacceptable, which means having to return the advance. Either way, the author's inability to execute the book will eventually be discovered, and it's much less painful for all concerned to assess this before entering into a contract.

Is more detail better for the annotated table of contents?

Yes and no. Sometimes I get proposals that have an annotated table of contents, and detailed chapter descriptions of several pages each, and two sample chapters. There's a sense of the material repeating itself, and that's counterproductive. Don't annotate so much that a sample chapter will seem like repetition. Annotate enough to show me you have thought through the full chapter—hit the highlights of what you plan to include, and make every sentence as interesting, provocative, insightful, or revelatory as you can.

How long should chapter descriptions be?

Could be a paragraph, could be several pages. But not both, as I mentioned before. Have some people read it and ask them to tell you where their attention wanders.

What kind of information is missing from the proposals you're sent?

I need any and all media information—magazine articles, TV and radio, is video available, were there reviews of previous books? Too often that is excluded or is too general to be helpful. I need to know of any public profile an author has—speeches, workshops, seminars, teaching, preaching, etc. What you did and for whom. This helps me understand what kind of outreach you have for book promotion. Authors must help sell their own books, and the life of the book is up to them once the publisher moves on to the next list. So personal outreach is important to develop.

Many people don't include blurb information. If the key researcher in the field was your dissertation advisor, tell me if you can get an endorsement from that person. Any authors, public figures, or important movers and shakers in the subject area whom you know and might be able to ask for a blurb are good for me to know about.

All of this information increases the potential value of your project to the publisher. Knowing it up front expedites the editor's response to the material. It also tells the editor you have done your homework about the requirements of the industry, so you won't be using your own book as learning experience at the publisher's expense.

What's the kiss of death in book proposals?

I don't let anything interfere with my reading of the proposal if the idea interests me. But there's a lot that betrays ignorance and makes the author look foolish, which obviously you'd want to avoid. I chuckle when I see statements such as "the author would be willing to make himself available for book tours and appearances on national television." This shows lack of knowledge of the industry—many authors don't get tours, and those who do are considered lucky. It's not a matter of the author being willing to go on tour; it's more a matter of the publisher being willing to pay for it. It is smarter to show the publisher how you are laying groundwork for your own promotional efforts, how your previous experiences have given you public exposure or ease in such situations. Give details on how you plan to expand your personal profile to maximize book sales. The hope is that the publisher will decide that a tour would be a worthwhile investment in you and your book.

What was your most memorable proposal?
A proposal composed entirely of words with the letter *R*.

Wendy Hubbert, Jeremy P. Tarcher, Inc.

How important is the market information provided by the author?

Usually it's very important. We are marketing generalists, and we look upon the author as a marketing specialist in his or her area. A really salable nonfiction idea generally has a clearly targeted audience, and we can use all the help we can get in identifying that audience, first, as editors pitching the book to an editorial board, second, as editors coordinating a publishing plan, third, as publishers pitching the book to the sales force, and fourth, as sales reps pitching the book to booksellers. It's less important for fiction or for non-category nonfiction.

For those books, what's more important is a feel for the audience, for example: "For the two million readers of *Midnight In The Garden Of Good And Evil* and *Into the Wild,* this is a book about a young man's struggle to survive, and his mysterious and tragic death in the swampy wilds around Savannah."

What do you like to see in the way of market research?

Real concrete information. None of this "Millions of people will want this book because it's a really good book" hooey. Numbers. "There are 35 million owners of pet dogs in this country and they spend *$XX* per year on books." What does the audience for this book read? What do they watch on TV? Other books they bought—with sales figures. Comparative titles and sales information. Any marketing and publicity information the author, as the market specialist, knows about that we don't. If it's a fishing book, and the author knows that Sally Jessy Raphael is a huge fishing fan, that's important. Is this an issue that's been gathering media steam lately? How can we best reach this market, publicity and promotion-wise?

How accurate is that information usually?

In the really good proposals, it's pretty tight, thorough, and accurate. In bad ones, it's usually hot air.

For a typical nonfiction proposal do you usually want to see a sample chapter?

Yes.

Do you read that sample chapter?

If it's a good proposal and a good idea, yes. If it's a good idea with an author who doesn't seem to be much of an authority, yes. If it's a bad idea, no.

What does the sample chapter tell you?

Can the author write? Express the concept clearly, colorfully, engagingly, provocatively? Does the concept hold up to expanded exploration, or is it really just a magazine article? What's the tone, the approach? Is it too fluffy or too academic?

When can an author not include a sample chapter?

If what the publisher is buying is a celebrity or an authority who's written numerous other books, or if it's a book idea with the understanding that a writer will be put on the project later, or if the project is so huge and hot that it's being sold on the basis of a verbal discussion or letter proposal.

As far as the annotated table of contents goes, is more detail better?

Again, it depends. You want to see a plain table of contents, to get a bird's-eye view of the book. You also want to see a thumbnail of each chapter. It never hurts to go into some detail on the chapters, though, because it shows the author has thoroughly thought through the book. But too much detail in an annotated table of contents makes the reader of the proposal lose the train of thought of the book as a whole.

How long should each chapter description be?

Not that long—just enough to give the editor a thorough sense of what's in the chapter without making him or her lose the sense of the book as a whole. A paragraph, I'd say. But remember this is in conjunction with a sample chapter and an overview of the book and a plain table of contents. Each of these things shows the book from a slightly different angle, so the editor winds up with a complete, three-dimensional sense of the book and how the author has thought it through.

What kind of information is missing from the proposals you're sent?

Usually marketing information, and information about the author presented in a way that's relevant to the publisher. For example, what I want to see in an author bio is, where does that person give lectures and seminars? How many a year (or a month or a week)? How many people attend? If we published this book, what could the author do to reach the market with a publisher's help? Don't talk about what the publisher could do ("You could get me on *Oprah,* where I'd be really interesting"), but "My contact at *Self* magazine has promised me an excerpt to coincide with publication" or "Iams pet food company has said they will buy 500 copies of the book for premium sales." These are leads that we're well equipped to follow up. What's usually missing is a sense that the author understands how marketing and promotion works these days, and understands how they can act as the promotional bloodhound for their book and *use* the publisher effectively— presenting an opportunity to the publisher as a win-win opportunity that just needs to be followed up on and executed, rather than putting all that energy into a blanket complaint about the lack of personal attention their book gets.

What are the most common mistakes made in book proposals?

Telling publishers how to do their job. There's a fine line between convincing the publisher you have a solid vision of your book and being so strong about that vision that the publisher wonders what they're needed for. This means you can say, "My book should be small format hardcover," but not "This book will be a hardcover, five and three-eighths by eight and one-quarter inches, with full color illustrations throughout." Another mistake is not doing research. When you're coming up with marketing ideas, try to have a clue about how publishing works so you don't say things like, "Publicity for this book can include a full-page ad in *The New York Times* and front-of-store display at B&N" or "I'd be happy to go on a ten-city author tour." Let the publicity and advertising departments do what they know how to do, and stick to what you know how to do, like making use of print, radio, or TV contacts and reaching your market at a grassroots level or through nontraditional outlets.

In your opinion, what should never be said in a book proposal?

Would you talk about money at an initial job interview? The kinds of authors I like to work with wouldn't. Saying things like "I need a ten thousand dollar permissions budget" is a huge turn-off. In general, I wish authors would approach proposals more as they'd approach a job interview. "I need this job, and this job needs me. How do I convince the publisher that I'll be an effective addition to their team?" Not "What can the publisher do for me?" but "What can I do for the publisher to help them effectively sell my book?"

What constitutes the kiss of death for a book proposal?

"There's no competition for this book" or "This book is a guaranteed bestseller," for example. Typos. Any indication that the author is going to be difficult. Derogatory remarks about their previous publisher—that's a bad sign.

Can you tell me about your most memorable proposals?

You tend not to remember the bad ones, so the memorable ones are also the best ones. Truly memorable proposals are the ones where all the elements come together. They're head and shoulders above the pack. The idea is amazing, the author's credentials are perfect, the voice is dead-on, the writing is stellar. These are proposals that you're itching to publish as soon as you start to read them. You almost can't bear to finish reading the proposal because it just keeps getting better and better and you don't want to get too attached in case someone won't let you publish the book.

What were your best proposals? Worst proposals?

Bad proposals are those that basically say this book will be a bestseller off the front counters of bookstores. This raises editorial hackles on so many levels—the author doesn't know how much money we waste trying to get bookstores to use counter displays, doesn't know how limited the counter space is in bookstores. His is clearly the kind of book that has no target market—it's an "impulse buy" for the general public. As such, it should speak for itself—that's the kind of book that should show how funny and clever and timely it is, rather than having its author tell the publisher all of the above.

John Bell, Addison-Wesley

How important is the author's market research?

I don't look at an author's market research in the same way that, say, a bank lending officer looks at the marketing section of a business plan. The publisher will do the retail marketing, after all. More important than the author's actual findings is whether he or she identifies opportunities that ring true.

I read between the lines to find answers to questions like these: Does the author understand the dynamic of publishers selling books to stores (a thirty-second sales pitch)? Of stores selling to customers (every book has to go on one category shelf)? Does he or she understand why readers buy books, why journalists run stories? Does he or she bring a knowledge of the associations, Internet newsgroups, and other groups working in this field? A proposal can list a vast array of selling and media outlets without showing a good grasp of real opportunities and real obstacles.

One sad irony: Authors are usually bookstore customers, so they have useful experience. Sometimes they seem to forget that knowledge when they're thinking of who will buy their book, and how. If they think ads will sell the book, when was the last time *they* bought a book because of an ad? If they think a book should be shelved in, say, both "automotive" and "personal finance," have they seen stores treat other titles that way?

On some types of books, especially in business, it's also helpful to see markets the author can reach outside of stores: training classes, special sales to organizations, schools, speaking audiences, etc. The specifics of an author's speaking engagements in the past year, client list, meeting attendance, and the like are important. This is one area where the author takes the marketing lead.

Do you read the sample chapter?

I always read the sample chapter. It's the only piece of a proposal that shows the look and feel that the author envisions for the book. The rare time I don't expect to see a sample chapter is when the author has written a long article on the topic. In some cases, such an article shows the right writing style, tone, approach, and other qualities I look for in a sample chapter. (In other cases, it doesn't leave me wanting to know more—the "more" being in book form.)

What should be in the annotated table of contents?

The chapter summary is crucial—it's the heart of a book proposal. I expect to see between one long to four medium paragraphs per chapter, showing how the book's argument or narrative develops.

In a book based on the information model, many chapters could have the same structure. For instance, a book on common childhood illnesses could have chapters on mumps, measles, rubella, etc., with the same sections in each: duration, visible symptoms, and so forth. In this case, a single detailed chapter summary showing how the structure works and a list of the topics of the other chapters is enough.

It's better to give away secrets in the chapter summary than to leave proposal readers guessing about what you mean, or feeling lukewarm by such promises as "This chapter closes by explaining the Six Secrets of Successful Sleep." The chapter summary is also what the marketers evaluate to see how they can pitch the book—indeed, depending on the publishing schedule, it may be what they use to create the initial marketing materials! Captivate us with your information. Tell us something we don't know.

What's commonly missing information in book proposals?

Sales figures for previous books. If we don't see that data, we assume sales were not just average but dismal. Reviews are good to include, but in today's computerized retailing climate, they can't substitute for sales.

Different titles inside and out indicate unsettled thinking by either the author or agent or both. Since a publisher wants input into the title anyway, the proposal title needn't be perfect; it needs only to be good enough for the task of selling the project.

Lists of competing titles often miss important books. Nevertheless, it's more important to recognize the category leaders and the reasons they're successful than to exhaustively run down every title. Again, bookstore shopping experience helps. To be really sneaky, check out the lists of the publishers you're submitting to for competition; editors know competing titles on their own lists even if no one bought those books.

Some proposals come without cover letters—that's unprofessional.

Finally, if you're lucky enough to have talked with an editor about your project, don't assume you needn't repeat what you said. The editor will be trying to convince his or her colleagues that your proposal is worthy, so provide all the fuel needed for that effort. Write for total strangers. Write for a meeting at which your editor has laryngitis. Try to make the project sell itself.

What are instant turn-offs?

Misspelling *foreword* as *forward*. Writing, "This book will interest everyone who has a job [or any other generalization just as sweeping]." There are100+ million people with jobs in the U.S., and a *very* big book sells a million copies. Do the math, and you realize that no book ever interests that whole market. Writing, "Tom Peters [or some other big name author] will be approached to write a foreword." In *Henry IV, Part II,* after Owen Glendower claims he can call up spirits, Hotspur replies, "So can I. So can any man. But do they come when you do call them?" Show some evidence that a name author will actually respond to such an invitation, or name-dropping hurts. Writing, "My last book failed because the publisher didn't market it." Sure, this is sometimes true. But putting the blame on your previous publisher mainly serves to show that you were part of an ineffective team effort, when what you want to show is that you know how to be a supportive partner in your future endeavors. Also, "I read it to my wife and kids, and they liked it." This could mean you've got a good manuscript; it could equally well mean you've got a good wife and kids.

Judy Brief, McGraw-Hill Computer Books

What do you expect to see in the overview section of a proposal?
The writer should answer these questions: Why do you feel compelled to write this book? Why will someone want to read it? Is there a particularly timely nature of the subject area? What are the specific benefits of your book? These will be key selling points, so be precise.

What about the market section?
Tell me who will be the audience for this title. Try to avoid falling into the "all things for all people" trap. Specify who will need to read this book, citing job titles and identifying industries. Include information on professional associations, potential courses, and any other items that may help us reach your audience.

What about the competition section?
List other books on the same or related subjects that have been written for the same market. Include all pertinent information (author, title,

publisher, date published, price, and number of pages). Then provide a sentence or two to explain how your book is different from, and, of course, better than, each.

What about the annotated table of contents?

Describe the contents of your book in commonly understood language. Be as precise as possible, providing a rundown of subjects treated in detail. Indicate how in-depth your coverage will be.

What about manuscript details?

The author should estimate the number of pages in the book and say approximately how many illustrations will be included and answer some other questions. Can the illustrations be black and white, or is color necessary? How long will it take you to complete the entire manuscript? Is the book tied to any software release? Will the work require any add-ons such as a disk or CD-ROM?

What about an author bio?

Yes—we'd like to get to know you. Please include a recent résumé, as well as a list of professional affiliations. Are you a member of any associations related to the subject matter of the book?

Anything else you'd like to see?

It's helpful for the author to suggest some professional reviewers. While we may not use them, at times we find it helpful to have the names of one or two people whose expertise or reputation in your field will facilitate our evaluation process. These should not be close colleagues or friends, but peers whose opinions you would appreciate having. If possible, the author should provide addresses, phone numbers, and email addresses, too.

How much material do you require to make a decision on a proposed book?

Ideally, we'd love to see a finished manuscript. Therefore, please include as much material as you have already prepared, including a table of contents and any chapters you may have. If pertinent, it's also a good idea to enclose some illustrations if you can.

Laurie Abkemeier, Hyperion

How important is market information supplied by the author?
In terms of market research/information, it's only important if the topic of the book is very specific. For example, if it's a guide to lupus, then the first thing I'll want to know is how many people suffer from the disease and perhaps how many are projected to have it over the next five years. If it's a memoir about anorexia, I'll want to know how many people there are with eating disorders, although that won't be my main concern (the writing will be most important). If it's a guide to a TV show, all I care about is how many people watch the show. I never care whether or not the book would be a natural for course adoption or sell mainly in gift stores, because that's a minute part of the market we reach. I'm looking for: (*a*) a book that is in a category people buy anyway (self-help, how-to), or (*b*) a book that will get publicity and attention that will drive people to the bookstores.

What do you usually expect to see in a book proposal?
In a typical nonfiction proposal, I like to see a brief overview, a detailed table of contents (but preferably one that fits on one page for easy reference in a meeting), and one to three sample chapters. Ninety percent of the time, I know if I'm going to want to acquire a book as soon as I hear the idea or read the cover letter. So I usually only read the sample chapters if my gut tells me there's something there for me. At the same time, I would never want an author or an agent not to send the sample chapters.

Is there anything you wish authors would *not* do?
My pet peeves include: agents who don't know when their client plans to complete the manuscript (haven't they talked about this?); no competition or comparison information at all; too much market

research (overkill); single-spaced proposals; proposals in fonts that are way too small or way too big or that have margins that are way too small or too big.

What's the kiss of death in book proposals?
1. Missing pages or duplicate pages.
2. Screwing up a book title or a best-selling author's name (Robert Paul Waller, for example).
3. In the competition discussion, trashing a bestseller—especially if it was one of ours!

This last one bears repeating. It is never necessary to trash the competition. All I care about is how the author's book will stand out, or why the author's book is similar to bestsellers and will therefore have many of the same buyers. It's especially good if you can combine two successful markets (people affected by anorexia plus people who read women's memoirs equals a big, big number!).

Linda Matthews and Cynthia Sherry, Chicago Review Press

How should unpublished authors approach your company?
First send a query letter with an SASE inside it. We will tell you on the basis of the letter whether we will read your proposal.

What about telephone calls?
Please don't call us to ask if we received your query or if we've read the proposal we requested from you. Include an SASE and you can be sure we will get back to you. It may take a month or so before you hear from us.

Briefly, what should go in the query letter?
The most important information in the query letter and in the proposal is a concise and accurate statement of what the book is. The second most important information is what competition exists for the

book. In the query letter, a brief statement is all that's needed. In the proposal, we want a thorough listing of competing titles, their authors, publishers, price, binding, pub date, and a one-sentence synopsis of the book's approach.

Anything else?

After listing the competition, be sure to explain concisely what your book has that the others do not. Don't just tell us that your book is "better," "different," or "more marketable"—prove it.

Is there anything you do *not* want to see?

Please don't spend pages telling us about mugs, aprons, and kitchen towels that could be marketed with your book, TV tie-ins you think would be terrific, or other marketing schemes for its sale. If you have some real contacts in the media world, tell us briefly what they are. Use the proposal to sell your *book* to us—that's what we will buy.

Do you require a sample chapter?

Always—and we read it carefully. We would much rather have a competent sample chapter than a long annotated table of contents. Our experience is that the sample chapter tells us what the author can do, and the contents tell us what he or she wishes or hopes to be able to do.

Any advice about the sample chapter?

Don't skimp on this part of the proposal. Don't let it read like a rough draft. We are using it to judge your skill and ability as a writer, as well as the viability of your idea.

Any other advice for authors?

When we call, be receptive to our thoughts about how the proposal could be reshaped to make it more salable, and if we ask you to rewrite it and you agree to do this, really do it. It's an investment of your time that will pay off for you when the book is accepted for publication. If we see that you have only half done what we asked for, that will kill your proposal for us.

Linda Reagan, Plenum Publishing

What do you like to see in a book proposal?

A useful book proposal should define in great detail the various markets for the book. What is the level of this book? Is this book aimed at both intelligent lay readers and professionals, or solely one or the other? Which types of individuals are likely to spend money on a book of this nature? Do any groups actually *need* this particular book? What is the competition for this book, and how will the proposed book fill a niche that the other books are missing?

What about an author bio?

Absolutely. The author should devote a paragraph to stating why he is uniquely qualified to write this particular book. He should name all newspapers, magazines, and journals that have quoted him, reviewed his past books, or published his pieces. I'd like clean copies of these articles with sources labeled—it enhances the presentation for me. For serious nonfiction, a complete résumé should be included as well.

What about a table of contents?

An extensive outline, rather than a bare bones table of contents, gives the editor a better understanding of the book's breadth, depth, and purpose. One paragraph per chapter, however, should suffice. In a letter, the author should state clearly and concisely his proposed thesis. The package should also include a sample chapter to demonstrate the author's singular knowledge, voice, and flair for writing, as well as an SASE.

Melissa Rosati, Routledge, Inc.

How important is the market information supplied by the author?

I'm impressed if the author knows the major trade organizations for his/her field. I'm *really* impressed if the author knows the membership, rate of growth, and mission of the organization. Also, what are the latest news stories or consumer trends about the subject? I like authors who can discuss the books they like and books they dislike in the specific category.

What do you want to see in the overview section?

I'm looking for some critical thought about the author's purpose. Why a book on this subject? What is new to say? What hasn't been said? Who (what customers) will care and why? In reality, I rarely get this information, so I usually ask for a revised proposal. If I get it, then I know the person is serious.

How important is the sample chapter?

A sample chapter is very important for first-time authors. If the author has a previously published book or magazine clippings, these are fine. I read for style. The author might be all over the place in terms of organization, but if I think the person conveys imagination and spirit for the topic, I'll solve the organizational problems.

What about a table of contents?

I do like an annotated table of contents because it shows me the author thought through the process of writing the book. The table of contents is really an outline. However, I don't rule a proposal out because it does not have a detailed TOC, but I usually do ask for one before I sign up a first-time author.

Is there anything that's the kiss of death in a proposal?

The only reason I reject a proposal outright is that it's not addressed to me or a specific person in the company—it's addressed, "Dear Sir." If the author doesn't take the time to call the company and ask for someone, I don't read it.

Kathy Welton, IDG Books

How should authors submit their proposals to IDG Books?

Your submission should consist of a cover letter introducing the project, an overview of the book, a detailed outline with chapter summaries, any marketing information you may have about the product or category of products you'll be writing about, any observations you have on competitive titles, and a brief author biography.

What about the cover letter?

The purpose of the cover letter is to introduce yourself and your proposal. The cover letter is a summary of the entire proposal and should highlight salient features of the manuscript you intend to write. Frequently, a well-written cover letter can make or break your proposal.

What should go into the overview section of the proposal?

The overview section describes the book that you envision. This part of the proposal is important, because it gives us an idea of your intended scope and your understanding of the subject. The overview should include a brief description of the [software] product or products that will serve as the focus of the [computer] book, as well as a description of how you will present the material on these products.

The overview should also explain why there is a need for a book on this topic. There may already be competing titles on the subject you wish to write on; if so, tell us how your book is different, why your approach is better, and what features you intend to include that will differentiate it from the others. We prefer that our books bring added value to the reader by providing inside tips, techniques to solve everyday problems, and advice about working with professionals. If you do intend to include electronic material or other multimedia material, please describe such material in a separate section and discuss why it enhances the proposed book.

What about the table of contents?

We ask that you provide a detailed outline or annotated table of contents at the time of the proposal. A narrative description of the parts and chapters you intend to include in the book is also important. We may receive more than one proposal on a particular topic—each of these could very well have similar outlines that delineate features of the product and how to use them. How *you* propose to discuss those features is what distinguishes your idea from others. We want to see your method of organization and how you plan your content to unfold. You are creating a scenario, not just a proposal, and you are telling us how and why you are presenting information to the reader. Why is it you want to make a certain point at a particular time? What will the reader get out of your method of presentation? We'll read your proposal like a director might read a screenplay—the dialogue, camera action, and props all combine to create a mental image.

What about sample material?

Several of our book series, for example, the *...For Dummies*™ series, require a certain style of writing and format for presentation. If you're interested in writing for a specific line, we often request a writing sample that will show us you can write in the style of the book you are targeting.

What about market information?

You should also provide research information on the market you intend to write for. Include any information you have on the size of the market and the growth of interest in the topic. If you have read or heard estimates on product distribution, please quote your sources.

Also include any marketing material you may have about the topic you'll be writing about. If you're a consultant, for example, you may have information about the planned use of a particular product on a wide scale.

A book is a large investment on our part in time and money. We market our books extensively, and that's why we want as much information as possible about every book we publish. It's possible that you won't be able to tell us more than we already know, but information you provide can be used by sales and marketing to maximize the selling of your book.

What about the competition section?

We want you to produce a "best of class" book. You should be familiar with other titles in the subject area you are writing on, if there are any. Knowing how other writers present information, as well as the strengths and weaknesses of other titles, can benefit you in your planning. Keep in mind that book buyers who stock titles in bookstores are inundated with books. They're more likely to order and shelve a book that has a point of difference and a clear benefit over others.

What about an author bio?

You should provide any information about yourself that we can use to promote you as an "IDG expert author." Include any current or previous writing experience you have, books you have published, seminars you give, as well as pertinent positions you have held, and so on. We'd also like to know what other areas besides the one on which you are proposing to do a book you are knowledgeable in. Your proposal may be inappropriate for one subject but not for another.

Is there anything else you need to see?

Include an approximate page count with your table of contents or outline. A page estimation can help us determine how deeply you intend to go into the topic. One book page usually equals a single-spaced manuscript page if that page does not have art on it. If the page has a screen shot or illustration, calculate half of a single-spaced page.

Gene Brissie, Prentice Hall

How important is the market information supplied by the author?

Although almost every element of a proposal is important, I consider good marketing information essential. Verifiable numbers—when included—always help sway an editorial board ("There are X million people with diabetes in North America" or "Y million people bought used cars last year" or "There are 650,000 lawyers in the U.S."). And, as basic as that information sounds, it never hurts to include it, along with titles of competing books, prices, authors, publishers, and publication dates. If a proposal writer can supply real *sales* information about the competition, so much the better, even if it's just that the title *XYZ* is in its 23rd printing for Publisher *ABC* and has been a solid backlist title for nine years. There's no question, the last thing I want to see is the sentence, "There is no competition for this book." There always is.

What other proposal elements do you consider important, and why?

For our nonfiction proposals, we like to see a thorough table of contents and a writing sample. If we've worked with an author successfully in the past, we're usually willing to forgo the sample, but the table of contents is always necessary. We want to see where the writer is going, and, if we don't know the writer's work, we want to be sure he or she can get there. I think a good proposal should be five to twenty-five pages in length, demonstrate the author's knowledge of the subject, be grammatical and well written, and be double spaced with appropriate margins on white typing or printer paper. A good proposal is always a pleasure to read and a joy to present to an editorial board.

I find that we're much more willing to work with an author on making a proposal right for Prentice Hall if the proposal starts out well written to begin with. We bought a book last week which wasn't yet quite right for us simply because what the author had written was so good we knew we could help her shape it into the book we wanted.

Martha O'Sullivan, Que Corporation

How important is the market information supplied by the author?

Evidence of research is the number one thing I like to see in a book proposal. Although it's unrealistic to expect that an author can tailor a proposal for a particular series, I'd like the author to have done enough homework to suggest which series his proposal might fit into if we are interested in the idea. I don't want to take the risk of publishing a scattershot book.

However, market information from the author is not critical for us, because our publishing directors and our acquisitions editors are supposed to keep abreast of the industry. Usually the author's market information is fluff anyway.

What about the sample chapter?
I usually skim the sample chapter, but leave the final decision to our development staff. We require a sample for all new authors, as well as established authors aspiring to write for a new series. We basically look for adherence to our style and tone, especially for our *Using...* books and *Idiot's Guides.* For our *Ten-Minute Guides,* we look for the author's ability to complete lessons in ten minutes or less, which can often be difficult.

What should authors *not* do?
One of the most common mistakes is submitting a book proposal that does not remotely fit into our publishing plan. Again, a little homework will go a long way.

How much sample material do you need?
A good proposal should contain just an excerpt from the book, not the entire manuscript. Also, a general TOC (C-level outline, as we call it) is nice.

What were some of your most memorable proposals?
I've gotten far-out book proposals, such as how to teach your cat to use a mouse. I've also gotten good proposals that I can't use because we already have a similar book on the topic.

Charles Inlander, People's Medical Society

How important is the market information supplied by the author?
It's very important for us to gauge how well the author knows the market. It's important that market research, beyond the author's experience, be included in the proposal, as well as why that information

means the book will sell. It means that the author should not only have general market information, but also should show how comparable books have sold to that market. For example, it's easy to say 16 million people have diabetes, but then the author must show the sales figures (especially in trade editions) of similar books. We often reject proposals because we find out from other publishers that similar books did not do well.

What sort of information do you want to see in the author's market research?

Aside from what I've already mentioned, we want to see some age demographics as they relate to the topic. We know, for example, that people under forty are not big health book buyers unless it relates to fitness, diet, or children. Therefore, it's important for a proposal to tell us why older markets will buy the book and what information the author has that would back that up. We have found that most authors know very little about their would-be audience, which is why most books do not make money. We are small, and all of our books have to make money, so the market is as important as the topic, in many ways. Authors should figure out exactly the niche audience they want to write for, learn their buying characteristics, and the way they like to receive their information, and start from there. We've found that if your market research is accurate, the outcome is pretty good. However, we also understand that our definition of a big sell is much lower than what an author might anticipate. So, I think most responsible publishers probably feel a 10,000 hardback sell-through is pretty good, whereas an author is doing market research with the idea of selling 200,000 copies. That author's figure is drawn from misunderstanding the research, not the research itself.

Do you require a sample chapter?

We usually do want to see a sample chapter. It's important for several reasons: If this is a first-time author, the question is, can he or she write? Great minds and great ideas do not necessarily mean great writers. Sample chapters give us an idea of how well an author can put words to paper. Sample chapters also help us see if the author can say things effectively. Does he or she have a good "voice"? Does he know what he's talking about? Is the information all anecdotal or does it go beyond the author's small world of experience? We also like to meet with a potential author. Recently, we met with two co-authors who wrote a great proposal, great sample chapter, but argued with each other throughout our luncheon about issues that would need to be in the book. It was clear they could not agree on many things or work together well. It suggested to us that the one chapter probably took months to forge, and the proposal was probably written by their literary agent. We rejected their book though we really thought it had potential.

When do you *not* need a sample chapter?

Obviously, if we know the author well or have had experience with him or her, we don't need a sample chapter. Also, if the book is more reference than prose, we are more interested in a detailed content outline than a chapter.

What about the table of contents?

It's okay, but we have found most annotated tables of contents to be relatively useless to us. We prefer detailed chapter descriptions. A brief table of contents helps us understand the flow of the book, but the detailed chapter entries give us the real meat. We're always trying to find out if authors really do know what they're talking about and if they can break the topic up into logical divisions for the intended audience.

What's missing from proposals that you see?

Good market research is often missing—also, a detailed background statement—we like at least four or five pages—that sets up the topic. We want to know just what is so important that a book needs to be written about the subject. This background gives us a better sense of how the author reached the conclusion that a book will make a difference.

Is there something you think writers should avoid putting in a proposal?

The most common mistake we see in proposals is a recounting of the author's personal experience. For example, we receive a lot of proposals that are little more than a person wanting to tell their story. While it may be a good story, most people are not interested—everyone has a story to tell. The key is making one's story an example or inspiration for others.

Another mistake is taking what should be a magazine article at best and trying to make it into a book. Many proposals we receive are from people who really have about 2,000 to 3,000 words of new or important information to pass along. Their outlines and chapter descriptions are clearly stretching an already elastic point.

What shouldn't be put in a proposal?

Things that are not useful! Remember, a proposal is a sales kit. It should have everything needed to make me, the publisher, want to buy it. So leave out extraneous stuff. Don't show your ignorance by making wrong statements about your topic. This is quite common. For example, if you are writing about prescription drugs, you'd better include accurate data about the number dispensed each year, etc. We often see major errors of fact in proposals, which make us immediately reject them.

What's the kiss of death in a proposal?

Most of what I've already said, but I think the biggest kiss of death is when our editors are unable to figure out just what the point of it all is. In other words, a poorly organized, poorly written proposal will never be taken seriously, no matter how meritorious the subject.

What was your most memorable proposal?

My favorite proposal was one submitted by a physician and his lawyer son for a book called *How to Sue Your Doctor*. It seems this doctor had been sued many times by his patients and his son had defended him. It also seems that the doctor had won each case. Now they were going to use their experience to show how you could have beaten them! We rejected it.

Finally, let me add some additional comments. Our biggest disappointment is in most authors' inability to write clearly and logically. Having expertise in a subject is not good enough. Being able to communicate it on paper is the key. That's why we carefully scrutinize the writing ability of the author before we make a commitment, or we suggest that a credited coauthor be used. The coauthor must be a writer familiar with the subject. This is especially important with books giving advice or passing along information that a consumer will rely on.

We also look for topics that clearly bring something new to the table. That doesn't mean you can't write about arthritis, but do tell why your book is different from all the others out there—why your book will sell better.

Deborah Brody, Viking-Penguin

How important is market research supplied by the author?
Market research is important, but it shouldn't be exaggerated. Nothing makes me crazier than to have an author claim that everyone will want to read this book, and here are the reasons why each particular group of people will want to. It's just not true, and it's better to focus on being realistic. For example, don't pretend that Catholics are going to want to read a book on Passover, so they can "learn about history." Or that men will buy a book on weddings because "after all, they're half of the marriage."

Do you require a sample chapter?
I usually like to see a sample chapter, but it's not necessary if the author has published numerous books and writing samples are available. A sample chapter is most necessary to prove that the author can take an idea and actually write something. Anyone can do an annotated table of contents, but plenty of people have trouble with the real writing.

What about the table of contents?

I like a detailed table of contents—usually a paragraph or two about what will be included in each chapter.

What about the author bio?

That's crucial. Promotability is important, so the more there is about the author and his or her accomplishments and credentials, the better. I hate to say it, but if video is available, include it.

Anything else?

Yes—include favorable clippings about the author, relevant articles about the book's subject (if there was a *Time* magazine story or something like that), reviews of author's previous books, and early endorsements by known names.

What should an author *not* include?

An endorsement by a nobody is sort of pathetic.

What's the kiss of death for a proposal?

I really hate sloppiness. The kisses of death, for me, are typos, misspellings, and any obvious factual errors. The proposal must be really polished.

CHAPTER SEVEN

The Questions Literary Agents Are Most Often Asked

Do I need an agent?

Strictly speaking, no. This is hard for a literary agent to admit, but if you carefully target the publishers you query, and if your proposal is well written, well researched, and deals with marketable subject matter, your chances of selling it yourself are probably about the same as an agent's. However, agents do offer significant advantages when it comes to time and money. A good agent will know just who in the publishing industry is likely to be most receptive to your work and how to get that editor's attention far more efficiently than you could do on your own. An agent should be able to get you a better book contract, too.

How much do agents charge?

This varies from agent to agent. The standard in the industry these days is a 15 percent commission that comes out of the author's royalties from the book and from sales of everything related to the book, such as excerpted magazine articles, audio tapes, and films (but not speeches and personal appearances).

But there are variations on that theme. Some agents charge only 10 percent, but their number is dwindling. By now you have heard of agents who charge a reading fee just for looking at your work. Those agents typically make most of their money from fees and so have a vested interest in reading more manuscripts—not in getting the highest figure for those manuscripts that they do sell.

Many literary agencies make authors pay for all long distance phone calls made on their behalf, plus photocopying, messenger services, and other incidental expenses involved in getting the manuscript to publishers. These are costs you should ask about before you allow an agent to represent your work.

Still other agents don't work on commission; instead they review and market your proposal for an hourly fee, earning money regardless of whether they sell your proposal or not. Such an arrangement may be to the advantage of the well established author who is confident that publishers will buy his or her next book. By limiting the agent's fee to the amount of time the agent spends negotiating the sales contract, the writer is able to keep every dollar collected in royalties.

When agents are on commission, they also take a bite of subsequent sales of the book: typically, 20 percent commission on foreign sales, the higher figure being justified because they have to give a portion of their commission to the overseas agent.

Some agents are also "book packagers," agents who develop book ideas and then sell that idea (in the form of a proposal) to a publisher, with the understanding that the agent will find a suitable writer to bring the work to fruition. For this, these agents can receive up to a 50 percent commission. In some instances, the agent hires the writer for a flat fee (called "work for hire") and keeps all the royalties from sales.

What exactly does an agent do for this 15 percent?

Agents pitch your proposal or manuscript to publishers, try to get you the best deal, and negotiate your contract. They manage your business affairs with a publisher once the book is sold. A few agents actually edit their clients' book proposals and give other substantive assistance as the project is going forward. Again, the key is to find out what services that agent provides before he or she goes to work on your behalf. Many agents have their clients sign an agency agreement, a contract that spells out exactly what the agent's obligations are to the client and what are the rights of each side. One caution: Regardless of what the agent may tell you over the phone or in a meeting, it is the written contract that governs what you actually get. So if you don't see it in writing, don't expect the agent to make good on any promise, because it doesn't exist.

But why is an agent worth the 15 percent commission?

The answer to that question could take pages. But here is a short list of benefits a good agent can provide:

- An agent will edit or critique a book proposal before it is submitted, helping a good proposal evolve into a great one.
- Because agents have longstanding relationships with particular publishers and editors, an agent can sell a proposal faster than a writer can. Proposals submitted by agents go to the top of the pile on the editor's desk.
- Agents' familiarity with the publishing world lets them target book proposals to the most appropriate publishing companies.
- A literary agent's negotiating skills can (usually, but not always) get the writer at least a 15 percent larger advance, thus making the agent's commission immediately worthwhile.
- An agent does the tough negotiating with editors, so that the writer's relationship can be completely cordial.
- Agents know what clauses in a publisher's contract should be changed before the author signs. As more and more publishers become part of multinational corporations, publishing contracts are becoming vastly more complicated. There are plenty of issues to watch out for in a publishing contract: the advance, royalty rate (on gross or net?), option clause, subsidiary rights, foreign rights, cover art, copyright, the reserves-against-royalties clause, the audit provision, the out-of-print provision, freight pass-through provision, and who pays for future revisions, to name a few.

- Agents take care of all the business aspects of the writer-publisher relationship including: handling contract disputes, collecting money, getting money from publishers when it's overdue, reviewing royalty statements, and ensuring that publishers meet their contractual obligations. Agents relieve writers of most of the business worries, so that writers can do what writers do best: write.

- Agents are interested in writers' long-term success and provide valuable guidance (not to mention moral support) for their careers.

- Your agent will be there even if your book's editor leaves the publishing company. That's a comforting thought, because editors switch jobs all too often; your agent can bring the new editor up to speed on you and your book.

Agents who work on commission don't make money if they can't sell your proposal. They have a great incentive to get the best possible deal for your book.

What should I look for in an agent?

Some of the same things you look for in a spouse: trustworthiness and compatibility. Like marriage, an author-agent relationship is voluntary.

Financial stability is important. Agents are not immune to the vagaries of the economy. You want an agent who will still be in business even if bookselling falls into a slump.

Find out whether the agent works mainly with large, medium, or small publishers. An agent who has relationships with all three categories of publishers has an increased chance of selling any given book. Small publishers often are better at marketing certain kinds of books than large New York houses. Small publishers take a keen interest in everything they publish: They are less likely to let a book become "orphaned" once it's published (that is to say, left with no one at the company who is interested in its long-term prospects.) Large publishers, on the other hand, usually pay larger advances, offer more generous royalty rates, and can afford to spend on marketing and promotion (if they choose to). Some agents disdain to work with anything but the large houses, but some authors, especially the unpublished or those writing for specialized markets, might be better served by an agent who has close ties to some of the smaller publishing firms.

Look at the agent's track record. Who has the agent represented? Has the agent represented books similar to yours? Does this agent represent fiction, nonfiction, textbooks, articles, poetry? Keep in mind, though, that agents do not divulge how much they've made for other writers, because that information is confidential.

What is the agent's background? Nobody trains in college to become an agent. Of the approximately 600 literary agents in the United States, all did something else before becoming an agent.

Does the agent show a love for publishing? In other words, do you get a feeling that your agent-to-be loves his or her job?

How does the agency's printed agency material appear to you? Does this package inspire confidence in the agent's professionalism?

How should I approach an agent?

In a word: professionally. Everything you send to your prospective agent should look as neat and organized as you can make it. Be sure to include copies of previously published books or articles. Self-published books are of interest, too, but make sure you provide sales figures and information about sales outlets.

Most agents prefer the initial contact to be made in writing; after all, the written word is the stuff of the book business. Different agents have different policies about what they want to see in introductory submissions. For example, some agents want a one or two page letter; some want a cover letter with an outline and a sample chapter; some want the complete proposal, along with sample material; a few prefer to see the entire manuscript from a first-time author. Check the agent's policy before making any submission. (A phone call to the agency's office asking about the company's submission guidelines is an easy way to find out what the agent requires.) If the agent maintains a web site, you will likely find submission guidelines posted there.

If you are contacting an agent for the first time, without a personal reference from a current client, then do include a self-addressed stamped envelope for the agent's reply. It's okay to query several agents at once, but never make simultaneous manuscript submissions to more than one agent. Also in the never column: Never fax a proposal to an agent (unless invited to); never email anything that will take a long time (more than two or three minutes) to download to the agency's computer.

How long does it take for an agent to make a successful sale?

As with many things in publishing, that depends. Four to five weeks is the norm, but there are plenty of situations outside the norm. At certain points during the year, such as August, Thanksgiving, Christmas, publishers' sales conferences, and the annual Book Expo, the publishing world slows considerably. Also, most publishers use a committee to decide whether to make an offer on a book. This editorial board (called the "ed board" and made up of editors, company executives, and, in many cases, sales representatives) may meet only once a week, or once every two weeks. If your book looks as if it could pose legal problems, publishers might want their legal department to take a look at the proposal. All these factors can slow down the decision-making process.

Don't pressure an agent to get quick results on your proposal. It's a sign that you don't trust the agent. But even worse, if your agent, acting at your behest, keeps calling the publisher who is looking at your proposal, you send the message that you are impatient and possibly difficult to work with, and the publisher may well decide it's not worth the trouble of dealing with you to do your book.

Some book proposals take a long time to find the right publisher. Don't be discouraged by initial rejections—or even many rejections. The history of publishing is replete with stories of books that were rejected by dozens of publishers but later became bestsellers. As long as your agent has confidence in your proposal and in you, your book has the best chance for success.

Should I sign a contract with an agent?

Yes. It's best to lay out the terms of your relationship in writing. After all, this is a business relationship, and affairs that involve money should be spelled out on paper. Some agents want authors to sign contracts right away, at the first meeting; other agents need to have a signed contract only when they start sending the book around to publishers. Or the agent may want you to sign the contract before he or she reviews and edits the first draft of your proposal. Agents can offer single or multi-book contracts. If your agent doesn't offer a contract, at least get a letter of understanding, so that the important terms of your relationship are noted for the record.

What kind of advance will I get?

That's the most difficult question to answer. Typical book offers can range anywhere from zero to $100,000. Agents can't—and shouldn't—predict advances. If, on the one hand, the prediction is too high, the author becomes disenchanted with the result; if, on the other hand, the prediction is too low, the author begins to lose faith in the agent's professed knowledge about publishing.

The advance isn't necessarily the most important element of a publishing contract anyway. Under certain circumstances, the royalty schedule may be more significant than the advance. For example, a high advance coupled with a stingy royalty rate on a successful book may be worse than a low advance and a higher royalty rate.

What, then, is a good royalty rate?

That is another difficult question to answer (at least, succinctly). Most royalty rates are on a sliding scale, escalating as the sales of books increase. Hardcover royalty rates are often 10 percent of the listed retail price for the first 10,000 copies sold; 12½ percent for the next 5,000 copies; and 15 percent thereafter. Trade paperback rates may be as high, although more often they're lower in one or more ways. Trade paperback royalties may be based on net receipts, rather than gross receipts (that is, a percentage of the list price), or the royalty rate itself may be reduced, typically to about half the hardcover rate. Mass market paperback royalty rates might be 8 percent of the list price for the first 100,000 copies; then 10 pecent thereafter. Again, it depends on the publisher.

So far I've been talking about trade and mass market publishers only. Textbook, academic, and professional book publishers have their own systems for figuring royalties. Then there are those sales by trade and mass market publishers at what is known as "deep discount"— that means at a deeply reduced royalty rate, which occurs when large quantities of a book are sold to stores or wholesalers at more than half off the regular wholesale price. Mail order sales by the publisher have yet another, lower royalty rate.

Every publishing contract has to be scrutinized, and negotiated, to get the best possible royalty schedule for the author.

What if I don't like my agent, or I think the agent isn't doing enough to try to sell my book?

First, talk to your agent about the problem. If your conversation is unsatisfactory, and you have not signed a multi-book contract with the agent, you are free to end your relationship with that agent, in accordance with the termination clause of your contract. Agent-hopping has become rather commonplace in publishing these days. Your agent will have experienced author defections before. The principal downside of switching agents frequently is that you won't have an agent who's followed your long-term career course. Of course, if your agent doesn't seem to be concerned about your long-term prospects, that's a reason to leave.

There may be times you feel disappointed by your agent because he or she doesn't like a particular book proposal of yours. That is an acceptable and normal reaction. It's not in your interest, or the agent's, to submit a weak proposal to a publisher, because doing so will only damage your reputation. In these instances, it's worthwhile to at least listen to, if not heed, your agent's advice. But publishing is a subjective business, and you are free to take your idea elsewhere if your agent doesn't want to pursue it.

Most agency contracts require that you allow the agent sufficient time to sell your proposal once he or she has begun submitting it to publishers. However, most agents, if you ask, will gladly cease making any future submissions to publishers on your behalf.

Any time you lose faith in your agent, you should leave. Trust is the glue between authors and agents. Good agents want only satisfied clients, anyway.

One important point (one far too many clients fail to understand): Once the agent has already sold the book and you have signed a book contract with the publisher, you cannot retroactively fire your agent, at least as far as that book is concerned. The agent has done the work of making the sale and so has earned the commission for as long as the book remains in print. If your falling-out with your agent is so severe that you no longer trust the agent to handle the proceeds, then you may request that the publisher mail your royalties minus the agent's commission directly to you—and if the agent agrees to this settlement, the publisher should comply. But it would be unethical for you to attempt to deny the agent the commission for the book that he or she has successfully sold.

What if you fire your agent after he or she has contacted publishers on your behalf and then one of those publishers makes an offer you want to accept? Is the agent still due the commission? Courts of law that have considered this matter have generally found that the sale was due to the agent's efforts, and so commission must be paid. However, if you have retained a new agent, who has taken over the contract negotiations on your behalf, then every effort should be made to negotiate a fair split of the commission between the two agents who have both worked on the sale. Avoiding a protracted legal fight is nearly always advisable, for everyone's financial health.

What does an agent *not* do?

Agents can, at their option, choose to be many things to clients. Mostly, agents are a writer's business representative; they act to protect and promote a writer's best interests. Agents are not (usually) in the business of: teaching writing skills, rewriting substandard proposals into salable ones, lending writers money, being a writer's therapist, offering tax or general legal advice, being an answering service for clients, behaving as if any single writer is the agent's sole client, publicizing books, or taking calls at home.

An agent is a writer's most important ally. While an agent cannot be everything to a writer, he or she can make everything about the writing life (except the writing itself) more satisfying and rewarding.

How much time will I have to write the book?

That's something your agent negotiates for you—so be sure to tell your agent ahead of time how much time you want to write the manuscript, and include this information in the proposal. Sometimes a publisher may want a manuscript delivered sooner for marketing or other reasons; your agent will negotiate the due date in that case, consulting with you during the process.

I want to continue writing and editing for magazines part-time to keep myself current in the field. Is that a problem?

No. In fact, it's a good idea to continue to write for publications in your field—this keeps your name in the spotlight. Just be certain not to use anything that will appear in your book in another publication (unless the publisher has arranged for a magazine excerpt to help spur book sales).

How long will it be between when my manuscript is delivered and the book is published?

Publishers work in seasons—that is, books are published for a spring, summer, fall, or winter list, to coincide with the publisher's catalog, marketing pushes, and other quarterly events. (Some publishers have four seasons; others have just two or three.) So, if there's a short time between when you deliver your manuscript and the next publishing season, the publisher may wait until the following season before your book is published. Usually, it takes three to six months between when your manuscript is delivered and when it is published.

What is the typical first printing?

There is no "typical" first print run. First printings can range from as few as 2,000 copies to 200,000 and upwards. You can *estimate* what your first printing will be from the size of the advance: The larger the advance, the larger the first printing.

You Have a Book Publisher: Now What?

Negotiating Your Book Publishing Contract

Book publishing contracts are fraught with pitfalls for writers. As you would expect, contracts are written from the publisher's perspective and for the express purpose of financially benefiting the publisher.

Contracts are often the sum of a publisher's past mistakes and problems. If something went wrong in the past—a disappearing author or a messy libel suit, for example—the publisher will work a specific clause into future contracts to attempt to prevent a repeat occurrence.

Most of the time, the process of writing and publishing a book goes smoothly. Publishers recognize this, too, so they may be willing to be flexible about their contracts. But you do have to ask for the changes you want. Insist, if necessary. Otherwise, you will be stuck with a bad contract.

Here are some of the most egregious contract pitfalls that agents see. Your contract may or may not contain clauses with any of these writer-unfriendly features:

- Too low an advance. Advances should be on par with the author's talent and credentials, the amount of work involved, and reasonably anticipated sales.

- Too low or no percentage for subsidiary rights, which include magazine articles, films, audio tapes, foreign sales, book clubs, and electronic rights. The larger the percentage for the author, the better.

- Royalty rate too low. The larger the percentage, the better off the writer is. Publishers have two ways of calculating royalty rates: net and gross. Royalties paid on net are generally half of those paid on gross receipts (which is the list price of the book). Royalties should be paid on an escalating scale based on ever-higher sales levels that the book has reached. In other words, the author should be earning at a higher rate once the book has sold 7,500 copies, then higher still at 15,000 copies, and so on.

- Advance paid in slow increments. Sometimes publishers pay the advance in four, five, or six segments. The fewer payments the better for the author.

- Copyright in the publisher's name. The copyright should be in the author's name.

- Late penalties: Some publishers impose a draconian penalty for late delivery of the manuscript (or portion of the manuscript).

- No early delivery bonus. If there is a late penalty provision, there certainly should be an early delivery bonus!

- No requirement that the publisher accept or reject the manuscript within a given time period. Also, no requirement that the publisher must either publish the book within a given time or return to the author the rights to the unpublished work.

- A too-strict option clause. An option clause requires the author to submit his or her next proposal to the publisher for right of first refusal. Depending on how tightly it's worded, this clause can unduly limit the author's ability to pursue his or her craft.

- An overly broad noncompetition clause. Publishers don't want authors writing books on similar subjects, but authors need to write about what they know. If the noncompetition clause is too broadly worded, then almost anything else the author may produce could be interpreted as competing with the book under contract.

- No audit clause. Every publishing contract should give the author the chance to audit the publisher's financial records at least once a year.

- No bankruptcy clause. Publishers sometimes go belly up—what happens to you then? If a publisher goes bankrupt, the rights should revert to the author immediately.

- A strict reserve-against-returns clause. Publishers are permitted to hold back a certain percentage of the royalties against possible book returns from stores, but authors should try to limit the amount.

- A requirement that the author repay the publisher if the publisher cancels the book. When you've been working hard on a book according to the outline that the publisher accepted, and the company decides for its own reasons and through no fault of your own to cancel the book, it is only fair that you be allowed to keep any advance you were paid.

Carefully read through any contract that a publisher presents to you, searching for any or all of the problems described above. Remember, contracts, just like used cars, are meant to be negotiated. If you have an agent, let your agent play hardball for you. If there's a considerable sum of money involved, it will be worth your while to hire an attorney who specializes in publishing law to negotiate the contract for you. You will have to pay a retainer up front and pay for the attorney's time at the going rate per hour, but there will be no commission taken out of your advance or your royalties.

Agents are sometimes brought into the picture by clients at the stage of contract negotiations. The writer sends out the proposal unagented and secures a publisher without help but then signs on as a client once a book deal is in the works. An agent who has not sold the book for the client will typically receive a reduced commission, perhaps only half the standard 15 percent, for the work involved in negotiating the contract and managing the client's business with the publisher. Once the writer and the agent have established a working relationship, the agent usually will represent the client's subsequent books at the standard full commission.

Book Writing Guidelines

- Ask your publisher for a copy of their author guidelines.
- Find out what style manual, if any, your publisher uses. Get a copy and follow the style guidelines in that book. (This may save you from having to change every state name from "CT" to "Conn.," for example.)
- Call your editor and request a copy of a well-executed book that's similar to your book, published by your publisher.
- If you are uncertain about any technical aspects of your book, ask your editor. Questions you may want to ask include: Should you use footnotes, or endnotes, or should you incorporate all source information into the text? How many words from a particular source can be quoted without written permission? Is it okay to make up pseudonyms for people you have interviewed? Can you take the answers from two interview questions and edit them into one composite answer? How many pictures should be included? It's always best to have these questions answered early.
- If you have questions about the production process—from submitting the manuscript to approval of the final galleys—ask your own editor, the development editor, or copy editor. This is especially important if you are including illustrations.
- If you think you are going to be behind schedule, let your agent know right away. Ninety-nine percent of scheduling problems can be taken care of with a phone call, but it's important to alert your agent and editor the moment you suspect you're going to be late.
- Delivering your manuscript early is always all right (in fact, it's encouraged).

- It's much more effective to proofread on paper than on the computer screen.

- Always ask a friend or family member to proofread after you're finished. Two pair of eyes catch mistakes better than one pair.

- Back up your manuscript on two floppy disks; print the manuscript from time to time before it's finished; and keep a copy (or disk, or both) of the work-in-progress in another location such as @Backup, which I mentioned earlier.

- Let your agent take care of any problems that you are having or anticipate. Call your agent before you call your publisher.

- If you have a coauthor, always have a written collaboration agreement. Your agent can help you negotiate the collaboration agreement.

- Follow the outline you have submitted in your proposal as closely as possible. If your book is going to deviate substantially from the outline, check with your editor. Be especially attentive to length: If your book might be 20 percent longer or shorter than is estimated in your contract, talk with your editor before submitting the manuscript. Publishers plan the book's price based, in part, on the book's length.

- If possible, submit the first few chapters early, so you can get feedback on your style. Specifically ask your editor to review your chapters, and make the request in writing (otherwise your editor might just put the material aside until you submit the entire manuscript). It's easier to make a few changes as you go along than to have to make a large number of changes after you thought the book was finished.

- It generally takes thirty days from the time you submit your manuscript (or portions of your manuscript) before the publisher will cut your check.

Ask your editor when you can expect the edited manuscript back, and warn your publisher if you are planning a trip between the time you deliver the original manuscript and the book's publication date. After the edited manuscript comes back to you, you will need to review the changes requested and answer your editor's queries, a process that can take anywhere from a few hours to a few weeks. (This is also your last chance to make substantive changes of your own to the manuscript.) Later you will receive galleys to review and proofread.

Promoting Your Book

Eventually (assuming you follow all the wonderful advice you've received so far) your book *will* be published. Then what? Do you just sit around and wait for the royalty checks to pour in? No, nobody does that. To some extent, whether your book succeeds—or not—depends on your efforts.

I used to believe that publishers knew best—and did best—when it came to promoting books. Most publishers publicize their books—most of the time, but with differing degrees of enthusiasm and effectiveness.

I am convinced that it is no longer a matter of whether authors *should* promote their books, but *how* aggressively we should do so. My answer is "as aggressively as possible." Some publishers do absolutely nothing to promote their books, and if you, the author, don't take action, then your book's shelf life may fall somewhere between that of butter and yogurt (to paraphrase Calvin Trillin).

On the other hand, with some well-planned and -executed efforts on your part, your book may become a long-lived seller, rather than ending up in the recycling bin as some other publisher's source of cheap paper.

What to do then? Generalizing about promoting books has draw-backs, of course, because every book is different and requires its own special approach. So, as you read through my helpful hints (below), you'll be wise to consider your book's particular audience.

And that's a good place to start—your audience. Presumably your book is aimed at a particular market or markets. Perhaps it's aviation or parenting or health or travel or nature. The first thing you should do is to track down the magazines that are read by the people who will be reading your book. For example, if you've written a book about how to be a forgiving parent, then those magazines include *Parenting* and *Child*. If your book is about flying aces from World War II, then those magazines include World War II magazines, but also aviation publications like *Flying*.

But don't just send out a press release to those magazines. Find out the name of the editor who reviews books for them or who covers your book's specific subject for them within the general field. Unless your press release makes a soft landing on the desk of the person who is most likely to be interested in your book's subject, it's a good bet that the recipient will just toss your release into the nearest trash bin. So work the phones until you uncover the name—or names—of the right individuals at those magazines. Getting reviewed in a niche publication is well worth the effort, because people who subscribe to that magazine are already identified as avid readers of the exact sort of information your book will provide.

Next tackle the major newspapers. Again, it's important to send your press release to specific individuals, rather than "To the Editor" or "To Whom It May Concern." Most newspapers have editors for a variety of subjects—science, health, sports, lifestyle, travel, and so forth—so seek out the editor you think is best suited to your subject. Don't forget to send your press release to the book review editor, as well. But remember, there are many other places in the newspaper where your book can be reviewed.

Next are the radio stations—talk radio stations to be precise. Mail (or fax) your press release to as many as you can. That usually means purchasing a database of such stations that lists the shows and their producers or hosts. Alternatively, you could hire a public relations agency that already owns such a database, and have a professional send out the press releases for you (though this will be expensive). There are several good lists of radio talk shows, including the Gale directory. Although you may find a directory in the library, if you're really going to put yourself into the effort, I recommend that you purchase one. For each talk show you want to contact, enter the host's name, the station name, and the station's fax number into your computer's fax program and let your computer's fax program do the work overnight (when long distance rates are usually cheaper). Depending on your long distance company, you should figure it will cost about 20 cents for each station you fax.

Definitely contact all your local television stations that produce news and talk shows—and don't forget the cable channels. In each case find out the name of the producer who arranges author interviews or the reporter who covers the subject that you've written about, and mail or fax them your press release.

Pay particular attention to your local media. Writers always have a better shot at appearing in one of their local papers or on a local talk show than on one across the state or in some other state. In most big cities there is a plethora of small, sometimes free, community newspapers. These papers are often hungry for material, especially if that material is free.

What to send to the print media and TV and radio stations? For several reasons you *don't* want to send your book. (The publisher should pay for the shipping of the books.) First find out whether there's any interest, by sending a one- or two-page release that tells the recipient to call you (or a friend who will act as your assistant) to schedule an interview or receive a review copy. Pass along any requests for review copies to your publisher—they'll send them out at their expense. Whatever you do, don't tell the station to call you to schedule an interview and call the publisher for a copy of the book: That's two phone calls—too much work for most producers to bother about. One-stop shopping is what busy talk show producers say they prefer.

I haven't said anything about the national media—*Oprah, Today, Good Morning America, CBS This Morning,* the many different talk shows on CNN and the other cable and broadcast networks. There's no question—you should contact them all. Get the name of a producer at each show (they're generalists, so it doesn't matter which producer) and send them all a press release. With such a large number of shows on so many channels these days, and so much airtime to fill, there's a very good chance that you'll end up on at least one of them if your subject is intriguing enough.

A suggestion: You might have a better shot at getting on a show if you are pushing not just your own book but the ideas of a few other guests as well. Suggest opponents of your point of view who could be invited to appear along with you, to get a lively debate going. Producers like guests who can help them book the rest of the show. When my wife Peggy Robin talked to producers of *The Maury Povich Show* about appearing to plug her book on fertility treatment, she suggested two well-known figures who would ban such treatment as "unnatural," to speak for the other side. She also recommended some couples who were undergoing high tech reproductive treatments and one couple with their in-vitro-conceived triplets, to give the patients' point of view. The producers booked Peggy and all the suggested guests, resulting in an information-packed, high-energy hour—not the dry, jargon-laden show they had feared might result from an hour devoted to a medical topic.

One way to cut short the amount of time and effort you'll need to put into book promotion is to make use of any contacts you already may have among those in the media business. Look to friends, relatives, colleagues, or friends of friends who might be able to give you some leads and pointers. They may be glad to be asked. You would be surprised how hungry—sometimes desperate—reporters, television producers, and radio hosts are for ideas to help fill air time or newspaper column inches.

When you contact a producer, let that person know that you are available 24 hours a day. Never turn down a show, even if it's at 2:00 a.m. Not infrequently, it happens that shows receive last minute cancellations, and if the producer knows you are available, you may get a call.

Whatever else you do, you should saturate the media.

CHAPTER NINE

Sample Book Proposals

What follows are three complete sample book proposals—from actual books that Adler & Robin Books sold to publishers. The first is a health book by a magazine contributor who had not previously written a book. It contains all the sections of the proposal recommended in this guide. The second is a business book by an experienced book author with a long list of credits; his proposal, therefore, concentrates on selling the idea and detailing how the book will be structured; the publisher did not need a sample chapter to persuade him that the author could write the book. The third sample proposal is one of mine, for a parenting book.

Although you can learn a lot from examining the style, structure, and substance of each of these examples, remember, when it comes to crafting your own proposal, to take into account the particulars of your own unique project. It may work best for you, given the time and resources at your disposal, to expand one section—say, "The Market," and shorten or even omit, another—say, "The Competition," or the sample chapter. Always have an objective outsider review your proposal for mistakes and overall sense and tone before you send it out.

Your Second Pregnancy

Your Second Pregnancy:
What to Expect *This* Time

by Katie Tamony

Overview

Why a book for second-time pregnant moms? We all know why first-time pregnant women buy books—because they're going through a new experience, and it's exciting and frightening and strange all at once, and they're looking for guidance and reassurance from those who have been there. But doesn't the woman who has been through one pregnancy already know what to expect? Surprisingly, no. Second pregnancies are usually different from first pregnancies—and the woman suddenly finds herself experiencing signs and feelings that she never felt the first time around. Where does she turn for advice?

She can look things up in the books that she bought during her first pregnancy (that is, if she hasn't given them away to a pregnant friend, as so many women do)—but she'll find that those books were all written for the woman totally unfamiliar with the pregnancy experience. She already *knows* the basics, and the books have nothing to say about the unique questions she may have. Questions such as:

- Why am I not having morning sickness when I was sick at least twice a day during the first few months of my last pregnancy?

- When during my pregnancy is the best time to tell my child that we're having a baby?

- Why am I showing sooner and wearing maternity clothes before the fourth month?

- Should I have my older child attend a sibling preparation class—and should the child be present at the birth, remain in the waiting room, or stay home?

- Should I use the same OB as last time, or (since my first delivery was uncomplicated) this time use a nurse-midwife or consider having a home birth?

- Will my body undergo any permanent changes from this pregnancy, different from the changes that occurred in my first pregnancy?

- How can I take care of my family and still have time to recover during the postpartum period?

- If I had a cesarean the first time, will I have to have one again?

- If I had a vaginal birth the first time, does that mean I don't have to worry about having a cesarean this time?

- Is my risk of miscarriage higher or lower now that I've already had a baby?

- How can I fit a prenatal exercise routine into my day, now that I'm a working mother?

- Should I take a refresher course in Lamaze training?

- If I didn't breastfeed my first baby, should I try it this time around? Or, if I breastfed my first baby, would it be wrong for me not to do so with this one?

- Are there any complications that are more likely to occur in subsequent pregnancies?

- What if my first child comes down with chickenpox or flu while I'm pregnant?

- Will I get more stretch marks? Gain more weight? Lose weight more slowly than after the first birth?

There are hundreds more such questions. This book will answer them for all second-time mothers, and for third-, fourth-, and fifth-time mothers, too. Doctors reassuringly tell their patients that every pregnancy is different—but this book will tell you how and why!

The Market

Your Second Pregnancy will be particularly sought-after by those women who are having their second baby many years after their first one, a rapidly growing segment of society. When the last time you were pregnant was eight, ten, or twenty or maybe only two years ago, you forget a lot. Things change: New tests are introduced, new health hazards are discovered, and controversies you never heard of before must be addressed.

For example, in 1992, sonograms were given routinely. But in 1993, a study indicated that sonograms—for many women— were wasteful. Should you insist on one? *Your Second Pregnancy* answers this and explores other such controversies. Between your first and second pregnancies your OB may have moved, changed practices, or dropped out of the field altogether (because of the crisis of malpractice litigation in obstetrics today), so you may need to find a new one. You have changed, as well. You are no longer an anxious young woman waiting to hear the instructions of an older, wiser doctor. You have more of a sense of yourself, and you want to play a greater role in decisions about your prenatal care and childbirth procedures. This time around, you wish to hear the pros and cons of episiotomy, epidural anesthesia, and fetal monitoring before you make the decisions—not like last time, when you probably just went along with your doctor's recommendation.

Since second-time mothers are also more likely to be in their thirties, they also need a book that gives more attention to the complications that can develop in the older pregnant woman: gestational diabetes, preeclampsia, hypertension, toxemia, multiple gestation, and others.

Because the book is concerned with the needs of the pregnant woman who already has a child, it will also contain a section for mothers of adopted children who now find themselves pregnant for the first time. (*The New York Times,* December 26, 1991, Home section, page 1, reported on the increasing incidence of such families.)

Your Second Pregnancy will arrive at the time when it's most needed. The original baby boom generation born between 1946 and 1964 is aging, leaving behind the time of first childbearing. The birth rate has remained high and has been predicted to remain high for the next several years, as these women choose to have a second and occasionally a third or fourth child. It's becoming rare these days for families to choose to have more than three. So instead of being a frequent, commonplace occurrence in a woman's life, pregnancy has become an exceptional and very special experience. When a woman's second pregnancy may well be her last pregnancy, she would like to pay as much attention to what is happening to her body this time as she did the very first time.

There is no other source for second-time expectant moms to turn to. No other book on the market today occupies this particular niche. When women become pregnant with their second child, they can look and look for a book to guide them, but they will find nothing. Yes, a few other books cover a few of the questions that second-time mothers have—but there is no book written *specifically* for this very large (and growing) segment of the public.

About half of all women who become pregnant each year are having a second or later baby. **Many of these women are hungry for information that is written just for them**—that's abundantly clear from the letters received by *Parenting* magazine after my August 1993 cover story, "Pregnancy: The Second

Time Around." Here are some excerpts from the many letters the magazine received:

> I am excited to say I have definitely found the thrill and magic in my second pregnancy that was in your story, "Pregnancy: The Second Time Around."
>
> —Nancy, Lindsay, CA

> I was really happy to see someone take the time to write on the feelings of pregnancy the second time around. Thanks!
>
> —Nikki, Trout Run, PA

> Your article on second pregnancy was a welcome sight! Back pain and showing earlier are my *biggest* problems so far. Your tips for rest and gifts were great.
>
> —Judith, Lindenhurst, NY

> I have just finished reading your article, "Pregnancy: The Second Time Around," and I want to say THANK YOU! THANK YOU! THANK YOU! I didn't think anyone out there knew how I felt about this pregnancy. Your article made everything clear. I kept telling my husband that it's just not the same this time around.... Thank you very much for letting us "second timers" know someone really is thinking of us!
>
> —Lisa, Lake Elsinore, CA

> If only someone had told me how totally different my two pregnancies would have been, I think I would have waited a little bit longer! Thanks so much for a very informative piece, one I am sure that I will keep to pass on to friends who are working on baby number two.
>
> —Kathy, Medina, OH

Given current demographic trends, *Your Second Pregnancy* can be expected to be a strong seller for many years to come. It's enlightening to note that in 1959, 41 percent of Americans said that four was the ideal number of children to have, and two percent thought that two was the ideal number. (Roper surveys, 1959 and 1991). In 1991, just 10 percent said four, while 52 percent said that two was the ideal number of children to have. With fewer pregnancies, each pregnancy is more precious.

Additionally, the pregnancy rate for older women is increasing. Between 1980 and 1990, for women aged 35 to 39—a prime book buying group—the pregnancy rate increased 60 percent. For women 40 to 44, the pregnancy rate grew 41 percent.

Most telling from the perspective of potential sales is that 75 percent of births to women over 30 were second (or third) children.*

According to the U.S. Census Bureau, there will be between 3.9 and 4 million births a year in the U.S. through the year 2,000. Based on 2.1 children per family, that's a mean of 2,050,000 second (third or fourth, but primarily second) children per year. One demographic expert, Irma Zandl of the Zandl Group, a company that tracks family trends, says that parents—and mothers in particular—are showing more interest in children and pregnancies these days. "The idea of staying home with a baby is not considered a waste of time."

It's fact, not fiction, that women want as much information about their second pregnancy as possible. *American Demographics* writes: "The middle-class parent's seemingly infinite desire for education has created more diversity and breadth in childbirth classes. Books on pregnancy, childbirth, and baby names did very well in the 1980s and are still hot in the 1990s."

---

*"The Birth Business," American Demographics, September, 1993

The Competition

If *you* were pregnant with your second child, which would you buy: a new book about pregnancy or a book aimed at women having their second pregnancy?

What to Expect When You're Expecting (Workman) is a perennial bestseller (2.7 million sold since 1984). Clearly, many women pregnant with second children are buying the new version of this book (aimed primarily at the first-time pregnant woman who has little idea what to expect) because there is nothing written just for them. *Your Second Pregnancy* will give book buyers an attractive alternative when it comes time to buy a new pregnancy book.

Another strong seller, *Your Second Child* by Joan Solomon Weiss (Summit Books, 1981), appeals to second-time mothers but deals exclusively with childrearing issues after the new baby arrives. It has virtually nothing to say about the problems and questions of second-time pregnant women.

One book that has strong appeal for older pregnant women is *Pregnancy over 35* by Kathryn Shroetenboer-Cox (Ballantine Books), which has been selling well since its debut in 1989— but it has nothing to say to women under 35 who are expecting their second child. In fact, the primary audience for *Pregnancy over 35* is that small but growing percentage of women who are having their first child at a relatively advanced age.

There are also many books on the shelves about problem pregnancies, and these may interest the second-time expectant mother, who, because she may be older, is more at risk for complications; however, for the worried but basically healthy second-time expectant mother, these books just serve to increase anxiety. *Your Second Pregnancy* will answer common questions about the symptoms and complications in a down-to-earth way that will be very reassuring for most readers; for those few needing medical intervention, the book will arm them with medical information, allowing them to discuss their conditions knowledgeably with their doctors.

With *Your Second Pregnancy* on her bookshelf, the second-time pregnant mom will not have to track down the copies of her previously purchased pregnancy books that she lent to friends after her first pregnancy, nor will she need to buy replacements for the pregnancy books she sold at a yard sale or gave away to the fund-raising bazaar of her first child's nursery school.

About the Author

Katie Tamony is the author of "Pregnancy: The Second Time Around," the cover story of the August 1993 issue of *Parenting* magazine (circulation 900,000).

Katie is the former managing editor of *Northern California Home & Garden* magazine. A freelance journalist for the past two years, Katie has written articles for *Parenting, Practical Home-owner, Sunset, Peninsula,* and several other magazines. Her first article in *Parenting* appeared in 1991 and was called "First Days Back to Work." Katie graduated from the University of California at Berkeley.

She is the mother of two young daughters, Sara, three, and Caitlin, one-and-a-half. Katie and her family live in Redwood City, California.

Your Second Pregnancy

Annotated Table of Contents

Introduction

Why your second pregnancy won't be the same as your first. Why the concerns of second-time mothers are different from first-time mothers. The types of issues and choices you'll be facing during your pregnancy. How your pregnancy is likely to affect your family. How this book can help.

Chapter One—Congratulations! You're Pregnant ... Again!

Finding out you're pregnant. The early signs and symptoms (they'll be different this time around). Decisions about prenatal and obstetrical care. Pros and cons of sticking with your old OB, finding a new one, or choosing a nurse-midwife. Body changes during the first trimester (first twelve weeks). How to cope with first trimester fatigue and nausea—when you have to cope with your family's needs and your job, as well.

Chapter Two—Making Adjustments

Body changes during the second trimester. Second pregnancies mean earlier feeling of fetal movement and backache. Helping your child understand what is happening to Mommy. Prenatal nutrition for the busy mom. Dietary concerns: More second-timers drink coffee, tea, and soda, eat more fats, and generally watch their diet less carefully. Exercises for the woman who has no time for prenatal exercise class. Travel and vacations with your other child while you're pregnant. How to get enough sleep, the pregnant mom's ultimate reward.

Chapter Three—As the Due Date Looms Closer

Body changes during the third trimester. Common body image problems of later pregnancies: droopy breasts, stretch marks, spider veins, swollen ankles and feet, skin discoloration, etc. Birthing classes (Lamaze, Leboyer, etc.)—do you need a re-fresher course? Should you enroll your child in a sibling preparation class? Choosing a name—should you let your older child have a say?

Chapter Four—Problem Pregnancies

About gestational diabetes, preeclampsia, toxemia, preterm contractions, and other complications. Multiple gestation (twins, triplets, and more). Pregnancy and the over-30 mother. Tests and fetal diagnoses: alpha-fetoprotein, chorionic villae sampling, amniocentesis, and others.

Chapter Five—Playing It Safe

Why your child's favorite sandbox holds a threat to your fetus. Necessary precautions around outdoor cats, insects, pet turtles, and other animals. Dangers in raw meat, chicken, eggs, and fish, and other problems for the family meal-maker. Your pregnancy and your older child's illnesses (colds, flu, chickenpox, and other common diseases). How to avoid heavy lifting when your 40-pound first child demands to be carried.

Chapter Six—The Big Event

Labor and delivery—will it be easier this time around? Shorter? Less painful? Options for childbirth: episiotomy or not, anesthesia (and if so, what type), "rooming-in" (keeping your baby with you in your hospital room), what to do with your older child when you go into labor. Pros and cons of allowing your child to witness the birth.

Chapter Seven—Second Baby, Second Cesarean?

For those who had a cesarean last time around: Must you have one again? For those who had a vaginal delivery last time: What are the odds of cesarean delivery this time?

Chapter Eight—Getting Ready for a Major Change in Your Life

How another baby is likely to affect your family life—and how you can prepare for the changes that the new baby will bring.

Spacing between siblings. The new baby and your husband. Common anxieties in second pregnancies: that you can never love the new baby as much as you love your firstborn, that there will be "something wrong" with the next one, that you can't be lucky twice in a row, that your older child will always resent the baby (and you, for having it).

Chapter Nine—Making Room for Four (or Five or Six)

Strictly practical matters. Rearranging the furniture to make space for the baby. When the house hasn't grown to match the family's size, do you put the baby in with the older child, put it in the parents' room, or in the living room (pros and cons discussed)? Helping your toddler switch rooms (or give up the crib) without tears. Who's going to clean house and look after the older child while Mommy recovers from childbirth and is taking care of the newborn? The role of the extended family (grandparents, aunts, uncles, etc.).

Chapter Ten—The Feeding Decision

The problem of nursing a newborn when there's a recently weaned toddler in the house and other breastfeeding dilemmas of the second-time mother. Nursing your second child (when you bottlefed the first) or bottlefeeding the second child (when you breastfed the first). About working, mothering an older child, and taking care of a newborn.

Chapter Eleven—Sex and Gender

Sonograms and genetic testing now make it commonplace for parents to know in advance whether they'll be getting a boy or a girl. If you find out, should you tell your older child? Issues and concerns when the new baby is the same sex. Issues and concerns when the new baby is the opposite sex. When you'd been hoping for a boy and find out that you're getting a girl (or vice versa). Sexual intimacy in the lives of the expectant parents (if they can ever find the time!).

Chapter Twelve—Special Circumstances

When you're pregnant for the first time, but you have an older child by adoption. When your second child is by your new husband (a half-sibling to your older child). When your husband has older children and you are having your first baby.

Chapter Thirteen—Emotional Changes

There are a host of emotional differences between the first and second pregnancies. This final chapter seeks to answer some of them: Why am I more bored with this pregnancy? Why don't I feel as attached to this baby as I did with the first? Why is my husband aloof? My first child doesn't seem to comprehend the changes that are going to take place in his (or her) life and this makes me feel confused. I'm getting too little (or too much) attention from family and friends this time around.

Resource Guide

Suggested Reading List

Index

Sample Material

Katie Tamony's magazine article, "Your Second Pregnancy" from *Parenting* magazine, August 1993, was included in the proposal packet to provide a sense of the writing style and give a somewhat condensed example of how the subject matter would be handled in the eventual book.

Business Wisdom from the Talmud

By Larry Kahaner

> *The first question a person is asked at Judgment after death is "Did you deal in faith in your business?"*
>
> —Talmud, Bavli Shabbat, 31a

> *One who wishes to acquire wisdom should study the way money works, for there is no greater area of Torah study than this. It is like an overflowing stream.*
>
> —Talmud, Bava Batra, 175b

Overview

Victor Jacobs, the chief executive of Allou Health & Beauty Care, Inc., in Brooklyn, New York, is not an MBA, and he doesn't use B-school case studies to run his quarter of a billion-dollar company.

He and many other business owners rely on a much older management tool. In fact, they use the world's *oldest* source for business guidance: the Talmud.

The performance of this Talmud-based company is stellar. Since the pharmaceutical distribution company went public in 1989, sales have climbed from $71 million to almost $250 million and profits have quadrupled to $4 million. In a very low-margin business, Allou's 4.2 percent margins are double those of its closest competitors.

Without reservation, Jacobs credits the Talmud with his company's success: "It opens your mind and teaches you how to think. It gives you the best practical business advice anywhere."

The Talmud is the great compendium of Jewish law and lore. It's not just about religious matters, as many people may think. The Talmud (or "study") covers every aspect of life: medicine, raising children, astrology, law, food, religion, business, real estate, education, marital relationships, philosophy, mathematics—anything you can think of—and all in intricate detail.

Most important, the Talmud is about ethics, about handling everyday matters in a fair and just manner, according to a strict moral code. The Talmud is very clear and concise about how people should behave.

This is especially true in business matters. The Talmud lays down guidelines for running businesses, handling workers, buying and selling goods, forming partnerships, making agreements, paying taxes, and even advertising products. While ethical business practices are a reward unto themselves, the Talmud shows that operating a business in an ethical manner is good not only for the community at large but also for the company's bottom line.

These ethical and practical guidelines are as relevant today as they were thousands of years ago, and contemporary business leaders can learn a great deal from them.

Some Background on the Talmud

The Talmud is the written record of the oral commentary on the Torah (the Old Testament of the Bible; the literal translation of Torah is "teaching"), which had been repeated and memorized by Jews, and debated and discussed throughout the first Diaspora until they found homes and established settlements in Palestine and Babylonia around 500 C.E. It wasn't until the Jews felt secure enough in their new surroundings that they were willing to commit their teachings to paper (parchment, actually).

The Talmud is a collection of many different works from different periods. The Mishnah ("repetition") was the first codification of oral law compiled and edited by Rabbi Judah "the Prince" around 220 C.E. From the Mishnah rose the Gemara, which is a commentary on the Mishnah. We also begin to see a huge body of lore known as the Midrash and narrative lore known as the Aggadah. All of these combined layers make up what is known as the Talmud.

Because there were two centers of Jewish life in the ancient world, Palestine and Babylonia, two Talmuds were produced. The latter, the Babylonian Talmud, is the one most often quoted because it is larger and more comprehensive, about a half million words. The commentators often traveled between these two centers—the distances were not far—and so the texts are similar and not contradictory.

Who were these commentators? Over a period of hundreds of years, many men of varying backgrounds, experiences, and temperaments commented on the Torah, and their viewpoints have been included in the Talmud. There were people like Hillel, who was amiable and loved everybody, to the tempestuous Shammai, who stood at an opposite pole to Hillel. There was the warrior Akiba, who was instrumental in a quixotic revolt against Rome and died a martyr's death. You meet Simeon ben Shetach, known for his excruciating honesty, and Simeon ben Yohai, who devoted his commentary to mysticism in the Torah. Much of the lore of the Kabbalah is attributed to him.

All of these rabbis (a rabbi is not a holy person in the sense that a priest can be considered anointed; "rabbi" simply means "teacher") were working people, in touch with common wisdom. For example, Akiba was a shepherd, Rabbi Hiyya bar Abin was a carpenter, Rabbi Abba bar Zmina was a tailor, and Rabbi Yitzak Nafha was a blacksmith. They all esteemed manual labor, and this shows throughout the Talmud in its praise of hard work.

Their great diversity of thought and backgrounds gives the Talmud its rich texture. It also gives us a wide range of storytelling techniques: fables, parables, simple narration, dialogue, and allegory.

The layout of a page of Talmud shows this richness, too. In the middle of the page is the Torah passage. Around it are commentaries from various rabbis, which may go on for pages to expand on a single phrase.

Although the Talmud was written more than 1,500 years ago, the Torah and Mishnah have continued to be fair game for written commentators. Rashi interpreted the old rulings during the Middle Ages to take into account the new experience of life in Christian Europe. Likewise, Rabbi Moses Ben Maimon, more commonly known as Maimonides, tried to organize the Mishnah for the lay reader as well as for rabbis and judges. Most contemporary scholars study these latter-day commentators as part of their Talmudic study.

While the Talmud is bountiful, it can also seem sphinx-like and impenetrable. It is supposed to be accessible to everyone, but its very structure makes that difficult. Because it was originally an oral commentary, discussions go off on tangents, come back, wrap around, and go off again, as if you were having a conversation with another person. You will not find one section about business or another about money. These topics are scattered throughout the Talmud, and this, I believe, is what makes the Talmud inaccessible to most Westerners, who have been educated to think linearly. The Talmud has no such structure. Of course, this was necessary because these "thought-chains" were, for early Jews, a memory device to retain the material.

Rabbi Adin Steinsaltz, editor of the Talmud translation that bears his name (and a physicist by training), notes in the introduction to his Talmud: "The material of the Talmud was memorized and transmitted orally for centuries. Its ideas are joined to each other by inner links, and the order often reflects the need for memorization. Talmudic discourse shifts from one subject to a related subject or to a second that brings the first to mind in an associative way."

In ancient times Jews relied on the Talmud as their guide for everyday living because it covers every facet of life. Later, when Jews were segregated by authorities —outside of government control by the government's own choice—to their own towns (*shtetls* in Eastern Europe) or Jewish ghettos within Christian cities, the Talmud served as their only source of law and rules. In a sense, the Torah was like the Constitution of the United States, and the commenting rabbis were like the Supreme Court justices.

During the second Diaspora, when Jews were expelled from Spain in 1492 and scattered throughout Europe and the Mediterranean world, the Talmud kept Judaism together, binding Jews to the same ethical and moral values no matter where they lived. The Talmud made it possible for Judaism to adapt itself to every time and place, every kind of society, and every state of civilization. Clearly, any body of behavior and law that can keep a people connected despite their scattering has something of value for everyone, no matter what their religious beliefs.

It is not hyperbole to say that the Talmud is the very essence of Jewish life and is responsible for the survival of Jews, no matter how turbulent their surroundings.

This feat is even more remarkable because only two original Talmud manuscripts still remain intact—a Palestinian Talmud in Leyden, Holland and a Babylonian Talmud in Munich, Germany. During the Middle Ages, Talmuds were burned by church authorities and others who wanted to destroy Jewish belief and the religion. Bibles were largely left unharmed, because the Old Testament was considered the foundation of the New

Testament. Despite its burning and later wholesale censorship of the Talmud in Europe, the Talmud's teachings have survived and are followed by millions in our own time.

Who Needs *Business Wisdom from the Talmud*— and Why

The audience for this book is businesspeople who want practical and spiritual guidance rooted in concepts that have withstood time. Keep in mind that every religion that came after Judaism borrowed many of its precepts, especially the ethical tenets. The Torah is, after all, the world's oldest ethical document.

Indeed, one of the mainstays of Jewish tradition is that society has the right to enforce ethics and morality. You could call it "coerced morality"—though it makes some people uncomfortable to know that Judaism requires punishment for those who break society's rules. The belief that society has the right to force a moral code on its citizens is a particularly Jewish tenet.

This should come as no surprise, though. We sometimes forget that Judaic tenets were the first moral code to be introduced to the world. When Moses came down from Mount Sinai with the Ten Commandments, it was the first time that civilization had a code of ethics to which all were bound (no exceptions for the rulers or the wealthy). Before the Ten Commandments, there was no consistent moral code to govern human interaction. There were laws and regulations produced by rulers, but they were not of an ethical nature. They did not deal with *justice, fairness,* and *mercy*, which are the foundations of the Talmud.

Other Sources of Ancient Wisdom for Business People Today

There is a continued interest in the Talmud as evidenced by the success of the fifteen-volume *Steinsaltz Edition* by Random

House (more than 200,000 sold as of last fall) and the *Schottenstein Talmud* (with sales close to a half million copies as of last fall). This is part of an overall interest in using ancient, often religion-related texts to help solve modern problems and give advice. A good example is the excellent sales record of *Jesus: CEO* by Laurie Beth Jones (Hyperion, 1995), which shows how Jesus' ideas can be adapted by today's managers.

Although not about religion, Sun Tzu's *The Art of War* sells today in part because of modern interest in what the ancient sage had to say about competition and strategic planning. Another example is Machiavelli's *The Prince,* which has become standard reading in many business schools. In both these venerable works, precepts recognized for their depth and wisdom remain relevant to modern business practices.

As our modern business life becomes more complicated and difficult, we increasingly turn to the classics for guidance. We're beginning to understand that there is a good reason why these texts have survived so long: Their lessons work. As a society, we're also searching for spiritual guidance that has withstood the test of time.

In addition, there is growing awareness of ethical issues among corporate leaders. At last spring's White House Conference on Corporate Citizenship in Williamsburg, Virginia, attended by more than 100 CEOs of U.S. companies, the main topic was ethics—the relationship between corporations and workers and corporate responsibility. Attendees, including President Clinton, discussed issues that are all part of the Talmud's teachings. Of special interest to the President was the apparent unfair treatment of employees who have been laid off after years of dedicated service.

Recently we've seen pressure from groups such as the Interfaith Center on Corporate Responsibility which uses shareholder clout to move companies such as RJRNabisco, Kimberly-Clark, and GTE in a more ethical direction.

Why is it, then, that the Talmud and its powerful lessons have been largely ignored by many modern people—including many Jews? I suggest two reasons: First, that people believe the Talmud to be inaccessible—and without a layperson's guide such as *Business Wisdom from the Talmud,* it is. And second, because some Jews fear that any focus on Jewish success in business validates anti-Semitic stereotypes (the myth that "all Jews are rich" or that the religion is mainly concerned with the accumulation of wealth).

Steven Cohen, a demographer of American Jewish life, reports that one-third of American multimillionaires are Jewish, as are 40 to 50 percent of top earners in professions such as medicine, law, and the media. Some Jews prefer to downplay these figures, nervous that the stereotype of "the rich Jew who runs American business" will be reinforced. That worry fades, however, when you look at a 1976 *Harvard Business Review* study of 444 top executives of major U.S. corporations, which found that only 5 percent were Jewish. Cohen has updated his study, and this figure hasn't changed in 20 years.

I believe that the Talmud's teachings are precisely why Jews have been relatively successful in business and why they have attained high levels of achievement. This should be a cause for celebration—not denial.

Non-Jews as well as Jews can learn the business lessons of the Talmud—its wisdom is for everyone. Increasing public awareness of what the Talmud actually says will not only help break these stereotypical myths but also show that ethical behavior pays dividends.

How This Book Will Be Written

Business Wisdom from the Talmud will explain what the Talmud has to say about running companies ethically and successfully.

This book will cover issues relevant to modern businesses and discuss the answers found in Talmudic parables, sayings, stories, and allegories. The Talmud's lessons can teach today's business leaders its time-tested methods for management.

I will draw from commentaries by past and present scholars and current businesspeople. So far, I have secured the assistance of several Talmudic scholars, including Rabbi Pinchas Rosenstein, Director of the Jewish Association for Business Ethics in London, England, and Dr. Meir Tamari, who heads the Center for Business Ethics at the Jerusalem College of Technology, and businesspeople such as Victor Jacobs of Allou Health & Beauty Care, Inc. I also plan to solicit help from other Talmudic scholars and rabbis throughout the world.

Not only will I study texts and commentaries, but I plan to use powerful new tools such as the Talmud on CD-ROM, which permits keyword searches. This will allow me to find passages that may be difficult to locate otherwise.

Most important, this book will be written based on my careful reading of the Talmud, giving my interpretation of what it offers to modern business. As a business author and journalist for the past 20 years, I want to popularize the invaluable business lessons and concepts in the Talmud instead of keeping it in the rabbinical realm where it too often resides. The Talmud was not meant only for scholars; it was meant for everyone.

Synopis of Chapters in
Business Wisdom from the Talmud

Introduction
What is the Talmud? What Can Today's Business Leaders Learn from It?

This section will discuss the basics of the Talmud. I will show how the Talmud's ideas evolved from the Torah and its oral commentaries, and I will explain its importance to Jewish life and world history in general.

This book's focus will be on business ideas, ethics, and practical managing techniques, but I'll also give examples of how the Talmud handles other aspects of everyday life. I will show that the Talmud is a truly well-rounded guide to living. I will lay a strong foundation in the Introduction, so readers will understand that the Talmud gives practical information for all people, no matter what their religious beliefs. I'll show how these ideas have withstood the test of time, and are universal and applicable, no matter what the situation.

This section will introduce the Talmud's "personality." Although the Talmud always takes the high road in ethical matters, it takes into account the way society really works and how people are treated by others. The Talmud's authors can be downright cynical at times. For example, "He who has the money has the upper hand in law." It's not the kind of phrase we expect to read in a sacred work, but this particular observation is as true today as it was thousands of years ago. (Unfortunately, it probably will be true forever.)

Chapter 1
Why Do We Own Businesses? Why Do We Work?

Businesses exist to build wealth and supply work for people. You work to eat, and you build prosperous businesses so that you and others will have time for study, friends, and family relationships. The Talmud is pragmatic about the purpose of work and business. They are a means to an end. Yes, you should enjoy your work, but a business allows you to have food on your table and helps others do the same.

The Talmud stresses the importance of running businesses in a hard-nosed and profitable manner. Allou Health & Beauty Inc.'s Jacobs adheres to the Talmud's admonition: "Buying and selling doesn't make you a businessman." Jacobs explains, "If I can't make dollars, I am not interested in volume." While most wholesalers focus on volume and compensate their sales force based on production, Allou's thirty salespeople work on an incentive system that rewards profitability. Each salesperson tracks client accounts and calculates the gross margins of every transaction. Salespeople are allowed to offer discounts, but if their average gross margins drop below the set guidelines, their commissions are trimmed.

A company should fill a particular need. It should give consumers a product or service that is wanted and necessary. The Talmud states, "He performed no evil against his fellow man, namely he began no competitive enterprise or trade where there was no demand for it."

This passage has a double meaning. First, it admonishes anyone whose business does not fulfill a need. To do otherwise is a useless exercise (and poor business sense). Second, it prohibits starting a business simply to put another company out of business, to take away their market without giving extra value to their customers. The Talmud's commentators looked down on anyone who opened a store in a village that could support only one establishment.

Work is imperative in one's life. The rabbis all praised labor, especially manual labor, and this idea shows up constantly in the Talmud. Rabbi Simeon used to carry baskets on his shoulder. He was a day laborer. When asked by students why he worked so hard when he could have taught for money, he replied, "Great is labor, for it honors the laborer."

Learning a trade or skill has always been part of the Jewish tradition, and you see it in the Talmud: "He who does not teach his son an occupation is as one who has taught his son to rob," says one passage. Another warns, "Though the famine lasted seven years, it never so muoh as passed the craftsman's door."

Sometimes, the time and effort it takes to accumulate money can interfere with living a full and righteous life. If all you do is work, then you have no time to study the Talmud, which is more important. This is also the basis of the Jewish tradition of education. While you are encouraged to work hard and make money, it is also important to have time left over for study and family matters. The Talmud teaches that "enough is enough."

Lately, there have been newspaper and magazine articles about work-weary people ratcheting down their lives. They're working less, so that they can spend more time with their families, even if it means taking a cut in pay. Many people have decided to work from home to eliminate commuting time. Although the Talmud could not have predicted this trend, it contains a prescient statement: "Better to work close to home, even if it means a lower salary." The passage goes on to explain that a job that keeps you away from your family and community is an unnecessary burden.

Chapter 2
Wealth and Prosperity

One of the Talmud's basic teachings is that having wealth is a positive condition. Being rich is not a sin. Wealth does not make a person more or less worthy in the eyes of God. Unlike the preaching of Jesus and his disciples regarding the moral status of the poor, in Judaism poverty is not a virtue.

Poverty is to be avoided personally and also by nations because it leads to unsavory behavior. Rabbi Akiba noted, "The other nations when they are prosperous, honor their gods, but when misfortune befalls them, curse their gods." He goes on to explain that poverty causes nations to wage war, mistreat their citizens, and, of course, withhold prayers for their gods—a most grievous action.

Judaism teaches that with wealth comes great responsibility. Wealth and a profitable business are gifts from God. Judaism teaches that we are stewards of wealth for the relatively short time that we are living. Wealth may not be earned through theft, fraud, oppression, or by withholding information. Do Jews ever disobey these rules? Of course—witness the case of fallen financial wizard Michael Milken, who began reading the Talmud in prison, hoping to gain some ethical insights into his financial transgressions.

It may not be politically correct by today's standards, but the Talmud accepts that there will always be inequalities among people. There will be rich and poor, well-educated and ignorant, strong and weak.

However, the Talmud also says that those who are rich should give charity to the poor, those who are educated should teach the ignorant, and those who are strong should protect the weak. According to a 1994 Gallup Poll, Jews give more money to charity per capita than any other ethnic group. This is not surprising: The Talmud talks about charity a great deal in many different scenarios.

"In the scale of charity, the highest form is to hold a man who is falling and to keep him from falling and becoming a public charge by means of a gift, a loan, a partnership, or by finding him work. Such a man is like a load resting on the top of a wall; as long as it is in its place, one man can take hold of it and keep it there. But once he has fallen to the ground, five men cannot raise it up again." In this passage, we see the wisdom in taking care of things early, before they reach a critical stage. Quick fixes, often the way in business, are counterproductive in the long term.

Let's not forget one important item: self-interest. The Talmud understands the important role of self-interest, especially in business. Although self-interest can have a nasty connotation, it should be recognized as a necessary part of human nature. Without self-interest, companies cannot succeed. "But for the evil desire, no man would build a house or take a wife or have children or buy and sell in business," the Talmud states. However, although the Talmud understands and accepts self-interest, it also makes it clear that self-interest is never an excuse for unethical behavior.

Chapter 3
Employer-Employee Relationships

Employer-employee relationships, according to the Talmud, are agreements between free and independent people. All legal factors apply, and there is no relationship beyond the buying and selling of services. Therefore, there is nothing in the Talmud that precludes workers from striking, joining unions, and lobbying for their self-interest. They must do their best work for their pay, and recognize that it is partly their responsibility to see that the business is profitable and protected from fraud.

The Talmud forbids a worker from working a night job or any other activity if he will be too tired to give his primary employer a fair day's work. "A man must not plough with his ox at night and hire it out by day, nor must he work at his own affairs at night, and hire himself out by day." There is the story about a rabbi who visits a school and finds the teacher fatigued. His head is on the desk, his eyes are closed. The rabbi asks the cause and learns that the teacher has been fasting. He tells the man: "You are forbidden to act in this manner."

One of the most important lessons the 62-year-old Jacobs takes from the Talmud is this: "If you want to lose money, then you should not sit with your employees." In other words, management shouldn't be detached from labor—simple advice ignored by too many top managers. All members of the Jacobs family and top management have worked in almost every position in the company, from sales and buying to picking up orders and loading trucks. The elder Jacobs still spends most of his day roaming Allou's warehouse asking employees, "So, what's new?" This hearkens to the Talmud passage that also warns, "One who wishes to lose money should hire workers and not supervise them."

Owners are responsible to protect their interests, but they also are responsible for their employees' well-being. The overriding theme, as in most of the Talmud, is fairness—going beyond the letter of the law, if necessary, for this purpose.

In the Talmud there is a story of an employee who drops and breaks a glass object used in his work. Legally the employer is entitled to dock the wages of the employee for the value of this item. Since the employer in this example is relatively wealthy and the employee is quite poor, and the damage occurred through an accident, not through malice, it is better for the employer to forgive rather than dock the employee's wages. It is more important that "justice be served" than that the letter of the law be followed, and it would not be just for a wealthy employer to penalize a poor employee because of a mistake.

This story was played out in recent headlines: Aaron Feuerstein is a textile factory owner in Malden, Massachusetts. His factory, located in the Boston suburbs, burned to the ground just before Christmas. The 70-year-old owner, knowing full well that the factory would be closed for a long time during rebuilding, declared that his employees would continue to be paid during reconstruction. More than 1,400 employees were guaranteed their wages for a full 60 days and medical benefits for 90 days. "It was not the workers' fault that this happened," says Feuerstein. "But Jewish law, the Talmud, is very clear that I am responsible for their well-being. It is only fair."

This is an important concept to grasp if you want to be an ethical businessperson, and one that Feuerstein fully understood and implemented when his mill burned down.

Other subjects I will cover include executive compensation, disability insurance, worker's compensation, boycotts, and employee ownership of companies.

Chapter 4
Competition, Monopolies, and Free Trade

The Talmud tells the story of a tailor who comes to a village to make clothes and sell them. Instead of opening a store, he works from a pushcart in the town center. His low overhead allows him to charge rock-bottom prices. The other tailors, who are already in tight competition, waging price wars against each other, complain to the rabbis about this interloper whose prices are much lower. They claim that his entry into the community is unfair competition. The rabbis agree to act as arbiters using their interpretation of the Torah as their guide. These rulings later become part of the Talmud.

The rabbis rule that the Torah always encourages more entrants into a market, because competition makes prices fairer. Free enterprise is a mainstay of the Talmud. They also rule that the new tailor had broken no laws and should be allowed to continue his work.

They also rule, however, that he must pay an extra tax to equalize his costs with those of the store-bound merchants, because his business is using resources shared by everyone else, and so he must contribute his fair share to the community pool.

Although centuries old, the story could have been snatched from today's front page. In Washington, D.C. and other cities there has been an explosion of sidewalk vendors and subsequent complaints from nearby stores. Last year the D.C. City Council, in some apparent Talmudic thinking, decided that they would impose a special vendor tax to help even the playing field.

The Talmud also discusses the role of monopolies, oligopolies, and government-run businesses. In an age of increased privatization, the Talmud's discussions of government-operated businesses will prove useful for politicians thinking of turning over traditonally public tasks to private companies.

Chapter 5
Supply and Demand, Sellers' Rights, Buyers' Rights, Pricing, and Allowable Profits

These issues are extensively covered in the Talmud because the Talmud deals with the fairness of everyday buying and selling. Honesty is paramount: "The shopkeeper must wipe his measures twice a week, his weights once a week, and his scales every weighing."

The ancient Roman notion of *caveat emptor* or "Let the buyer beware," which was well accepted throughout the Roman

Empire, is not an acceptable way of doing business according to the Talmud. Each side—seller and buyer—has rights and responsibilities.

While the Talmud grants the buyer the right to make a profit, for example, the seller also has the right not to be gouged by the price. The rule established by the Talmud is this: "When a man profits, he should profit no more than one-sixth above his cost." On the other hand, the Talmud teaches that it is okay to be clever, even competitively cutthroat, in business matters. There is no sin in making money or being shrewd, as long as you do not deceive anyone.

The Talmud lets you know when to buy: "When merchandise is held in low esteem, its price at rock bottom, go and buy it up, for in the end its price will rise." This simple rule is followed by the world's savviest investors. Warren Buffett, for example, employs value investing. He looks for stocks that are undervalued and out of favor, unlike growth investors who buy stocks of growing companies.

Recent studies have shown that value investing has beaten growth investing over the long term. These traders might also follow the rule: "When merchandise is cheap, hasten to collect money and buy some." It can't be any clearer to modern ears: Buy low, sell high. But buyers should pay heed: "This is the way of traders; they show the inferior wares first and then display the best."

Buyers have rules to live by, too: Just as fraud pertains in buying and selling, so can it apply to spoken words. One may not say to a store owner, "How much does this item cost?" if he has no intention of buying it. Not only are you wasting the seller's time, but you are giving him false hope of making a sale.

Chapter 6
Agreements and Partnerships

All business agreements are governed by the Halakah, which is the Talmud's study of law. It covers all facets of the legal system from contracts to torts to criminal behavior. Many of our current-day legal practices come from the Talmud; for example, it's important to have witnesses to agreements, even if the two parties know each other to be trustworthy, as this story illustrates:

> Rabbi Ashi, the teacher of Rabina, sent a message to Rabina on Friday afternoon, asking him for a loan as a deposit on a piece of land. Rabina replied to the messenger, "Please prepare the documents and have witnesses." When Rabbi Ashi came, he asked, "Could you not even trust me?"

> "You especially I could not," answered Rabina. "Your mind is always full of the law, and you're more likely than someone else to forget the loan."

Beyond the legal regulations there are simple, down-to-earth lessons, for example: "A person should be a partner of one who is doing well; perhaps one should even do business with him, because everything he touches has a certain blessing." If businesses had followed this lesson in the 1980s, during the merger craze, many of the newly formed companies would not have been established. A *Fortune* magazine study showed that 75 percent of the mergers and acquisitions done in the 1980s were considered unsatisfactory by chief executives polled in the early 1990s. In the mid-1990s, many of these companies were split apart again.

Chapter 7
Banking and Finance: Interest, Loans, Credit, Taxation, and Financial Controls

The Talmud understands the workings of finance and investments. One of the hottest topics among Talmudic scholars these days is the collapse of Barings Bank. Market trader Nick Leeson, now serving six and a half years in Singapore's Changi Prison, made outrageous investments in derivatives without top management's knowledge and then hid the losses from them. He lied about his trades, saying they had been profitable.

Rabbi Pinchas Rosenstein, Director of the Jewish Association for Business Ethics in England, notes that the Talmud makes it very clear that financial controls should always be imposed on companies. In the case of Barings, financial controls were non-existent. The 27-year-old Leeson was allowed to control both the front and back offices, which led to abuse.

The Mishnah tells the story about the ancient priests who had to enter the Temple treasury without their usual sleeved cloaks, so as not to arouse any suspicion that they were secreting public funds in their oversized garments. "Even the greatest Jewish leader of all times, Moses, was expected to provide a full set of accounts relating to the raw materials donated for the construction of the tabernacle," says Rosenstein.

As a general business rule, the Talmud teaches you to diversify your investments. "A man should divide his money into three parts: one-third in land, one-third in merchandise, and one-third at hand [cash]." And in your business: "Your crops should be of three kinds: a third of the field in produce, another third in olives, and still another third in vines."

Taxation is thoroughly discussed in the Talmud. Halakhic law says that taxes must be levied with consent of the majority of the taxpayers and that they must be fair and equitable. Tax evasion is tantamount to theft from the community.

Loans are discussed at great length in the Talmud because of the Bible's prohibition on charging interest in most cases. I'll take up the issue of how Talmudic scholars tackled the matter of selling Israeli bonds, which are, of course, interest-paying debts.

Chapter 8
Corporate Responsibility to the Community: Charity, Welfare, Education, Environmental Issues, and Public Health

According to the Talmud, businesses have a responsibility for *what* they sell. "One is forbidden to sell heathens weapons of war. Nor may one sharpen their spears, or sell them knives, handcuffs, chains, bears, lions, or anything that can endanger the public. However, one may sell them shields which are only for defense."

In practical terms, this does not mean that selling weapons or dangerous items is forbidden. What it means is that you must be sure to whom you're selling them. For example, this law would prohibit the sale of alcohol to minors but not to adults (presuming the adult was responsible). This type of law is followed by many countries, including the United States, which refuse to sell weapons to terrorist nations. It's also the reasoning behind United Nations-sanctioned weapons embargoes against nations like Iraq while allowing the sale of medicines to these nations.

You might think that zoning and environmental issues are strictly modern concerns, but the Talmud was very precise about these matters centuries ago. "Graveyards and tanneries [which emit foul odors] are located at least 50 cubits [about 75 feet] outside a city. A tannery can only be operated on the east side of a city [because the prevailing winds will carry the bad odor away from the residential area]." On zoning, the Talmud notes, "If a person desires to open a shop in the courtyard, his neighbor may stop him because he will be kept awake by the noise of people going in and coming out of the shop."

I'll also cover topics such as welfare and minimum wage, as well as the role of companies in employee education and training.

Epilogue

The epilogue will summarize the main points of the book and emphasize the importance and usefulness of the Talmud to a nonsectarian audience. Although the Talmud was written by Jewish scholars for Jews, it bears repeating that anyone can benefit from its wisdom, whether they have a religious leaning or not.

I will also discuss the relationship of the Talmud to other religious literature such as the New Testament, the Koran, and the Book of Mormon. Every religion builds on the ones before. These works, which came after the Torah (Old Testament) and its commentaries, are built on the Talmud's lessons. I will show the Talmud's contributions to the ethical and practical tenets of all major religions.

This book will be about 75,000 words, with delivery in nine months.

About the Author

> *Wealth and riches are in his house, and his benevolence stands forever. This describes the man who writes excellent books and makes them available to others.*
>
> —Talmud, Ketubot, 50

Aside from my professional interest in business, I have a deeply personal reason for writing this book. I have been the primary researcher of the genealogy of my family, which I have been able to trace only to the early 1800s in the former principality of Galicia, once part of the Austro-Hungarian Empire. The area is now divided between Poland and Ukraine.

Before my family emigrated to the United States at the turn of the century, my last name was spelled Kahane (I believe I'm related to the late militant Rabbi Meir Kahane). The name Kahana is mentioned twice in the Talmud. He was one of the *amoraim* or translators of the Torah. This person's job was to listen to the Torah reader and translate and add commentary to the congregation about what was said. He held the job partly because he had a loud voice, and partly because he was a skilled interpreter of the Torah. It was these oral commentaries that became the Talmud. In writing this book, I like to think that I'm carrying on the traditions of my ancestors.

As a Jew, I was raised with little formal knowledge of the Talmud. It is only now, at age 46, that I have discovered its brilliance and practicality.

I have been a professional journalist for 20 years and am the author of seven nonfiction books, including: *Competitive Intelligence,* just published by Simon & Schuster; *Say It and Live It: The 50 Corporate Mission Statements That Hit the Mark* (co-author, Doubleday, 1995); *Cults That Kill* (Warner Books, 1989); and *On the Line: The Men of MCI Who Took on AT&T and Won* (Warner Books, 1987). I am a former Washington staff correspondent for *Business Week* magazine, a reporter for Knight-Ridder newspapers, and founding editor of *Communications Daily.*

I have written for numerous magazines, including *Omni, Wilderness Magazine, Presstime, Washingtonian, Washington Journalism Review, Popular Science, High Technology, Woman's World, American Bookseller, Sunbelt Executive, Management*

Technology, Consumers Digest, Physician's Management (currently senior contributing editor), *Telephony Magazine,* and *Fleet Owner* (currently Washington editor). I have also written for many newspapers, including *The Washington Post, The International Herald Tribune, The Christian Science Monitor,* and *Communications Week.* I am the recipient of an Associated Press Public Service Award for journalism.

I have appeared on many national TV and radio shows, including CNN's *Larry King Live, Evening Magazine,* CNBC's *Business Management,* National Public Radio's *All Things Considered,* and the *CBS Evening News.*

I am a licensed private investigator and president of KANE Associates International, a firm that specializes in intelligence gathering for corporate clients.

Tell Me a Fairy Tale: A Parent's Guide to Telling Magical and Mythical Stories

Tell Me a Fairy Tale
A Parent's Guide to Telling
Magical and Mythical Stories

by Bill Adler, Jr.

Overview

Is your three-year-old getting tired of hearing *Goldilocks* every evening? Are *you* getting tired of telling it? Do you wish you knew another fairy tale? And do you wish you had a quick and easy source for fairy tales?

Then *Tell Me a Fairy Tale: A Parent's Guide to Telling Magical and Mythical Stories* is the book of your dreams. *Tell Me a Fairy*

Tale contains summaries of fifty-one of the most popular children's fairy tales, fables, and legends. Each fairy tale condensation is no more than three pages, so it won't take longer than five minutes to get up to speed on any particular story.

Some of these stories are classic European fairy tales like *Little Red Riding Hood.* Others are classic American legends like *John Henry.* Others are from the African-American oral tradition, like *The Little Bird Grows.* Still others are from Native American cultures, like *The Little Scarred One.* Some of the tales are from distant lands—*Two of Everything* is Korean; *Casperl* is German. Each condensation contains:

- a brief summary of the story
- a description of the characters in the tale
- a plot description
- instructions for telling the tale.

Each tale will be accompanied by an illustration. The illustration isn't to show to your child (though you can); rather, its purpose is to give you a better sense of the flavor of the story. Many legends and fairy tales have rhymes; these will be included.

If you have ever used *Cliffs Notes,* you'll recognize the enormous potential and time-saving benefits of a book like *Tell Me a Fairy Tale.* Like *Cliffs Notes, Tell Me a Fairy Tale* is designed to help you remember and effectively recall important information— but, in this case, with your mission of thrilling and enrapturing your child.

The concept for this book came to me one evening when I discovered how very, very tired I was of telling *Goldilocks* to my two-and-a-half-year-old daughter, Karen. I had been doing so every night and naptime for nearly a year. While there was no real evidence that Karen was tiring of the tale, I was about to go mad. When, in the interest of my sanity, I skipped a part, like the business about sitting in the chairs, Karen was quick to insist, "The chairs, the chairs!"

If only I had known some other story to tell!

The problem was, I had neither the time nor the inclination to invest in the study of any of the volumes of collected fairy tales that can be found in any bookstore. For one thing, a complete collection would have been expensive and heavy to carry home from the store. For another, to sit and read page after page of a tale from such a book would take nearly half an hour each evening (and I knew Karen would never put up with leaving a tale unfinished for the next night). But, most importantly, it's much more enjoyable to *tell* a story than to read one—especially to a toddler. When you tell a story, there's unlimited flexibility; your imagination can illuminate the tale. Once you know the basic plot of a story, you can embellish it, or even personalize it to incorporate your child's own interests if you wish. Or you can shorten the story to hasten the advent of dreamtime.

The book will include an introduction that explains how to tell a fairy tale and how to change one to suit your fancy.

Tell Me a Fairy Tale is not a long book—deliberately so. *Tell Me a Fairy Tale* is meant to be unintimidating. Parents don't want to reread all the classic fairy tales and legends themselves; they just want to tell them for their children to enjoy. Keeping *Tell Me a Fairy Tale* short means that potential buyers won't be frightened away.

The Market

Parents, of course, are a huge, almost inexhaustible market for books that promise to make childrearing easier and more fun. Busy parents who have a limited amount of time to spend with their children are especially eager for books that can help them make the most of the time they do have—such as at bedtime. A recent poll proved this: When asked whether they would rather have a salary increase or more vacation time, most middle- and upper-middle-class Americans insist that they would rather have more time. Time to spend with their families, their children, at home. People joke about the term "quality time"—yet this is exactly what many of us seek. *Tell Me a Fairy Tale* helps satisfy that need.

Exactly who will buy *Tell Me a Fairy Tale*? An educated parent, male or female, who believes that his or her child deserves more than stale, ordinary, and often sexist fairy tales. These parents will typically be employed full-time and will have an urge to make the time spent with their children more enriching, and, at the same time, more enjoyable, for both parent and child.

How do these parents describe themselves? Smart, harried, successful, well-read (at least once upon a time, when they had time). These parents also admit that they have forgotten many fairy tales and are simply at a loss to tell their children anything other than mangled versions of *Goldilocks* or *Little Red Riding Hood.*

Tell Me a Fairy Tale is aimed at parents with children between the ages of one and eight years old. It fills an important market niche among parenting books.

The Competition

How to count the competition? There is plenty. Most of the competition, however, falls into one of two categories: anthologies of fairy tales or illustrated books of individual fairy tales. Nearly every major publisher has produced these two kinds of books. Books of both categories are too numerous to list here—they number in the hundreds—but it is apparent that they differ markedly from *Tell Me a Fairy Tale.* Look, for example, at *The Random House Book of Fairy Tales* (by Amy Erlich, $17.00, 205 pages, hardcover, Random House, 1985). This is a lovely book, as attested to by the fact that it's been in print since 1985. But it is typical of fairy tale anthologies: long stories, lavishly illustrated. Parents are supposed to *read* these stories, or children can read them on their own when they're old enough.

The Random House book contains all the expected, traditional tales. If you want to read less traditional children's stories, you have to hunt a little for an anthology like *Afro-American Folk Tales* (by Roger Abrahams, $15.00, 325 pages, cloth, Pantheon books, 1985.) Not all the stories in this book are meant for bedtime reading, as some are longer than the attention span of a typical child. But *Afro-American Folk Tales* is a good reference book, and it preserves some important stories. The same can be said for *Gypsy Folk Tales* (by Diane Tong, $12.95, 252 pages, paper, Harcourt Brace Jovanovich, 1989.) It's a valuable book, though not necessarily well-suited to the task of helping a young child drift off to dreamland.

There is an abundance of books that present a single fairy tale. Most of these range in price from about $4.95 for paperbacks to $19.95 for four-color illustrated books. These are books that parents read and show to their small children; in the hands of toddlers, though, these books don't last long.

Perhaps the most direct competition to *Tell Me a Fairy Tale* comes from Shari Lewis's *One-Minute Favorite Fairy Tales* ($3.99, 48 pages, paper, Dell, 1985). Shari Lewis, whose fame comes from the children's television program featuring the puppet Lamb Chop, has written a series of these books including, *One-Minute Bedtime Stories, One-Minute Animal Stories,* and *One-Minute Scary Stories*—thirteen in the series in all. These are terrific books, and are indeed competitive with *Tell Me a Fairy Tale.* But Shari Lewis's stories are meant to be *read,* while the stories in *Tell Me a Fairy Tale* are meant to be *told.* The stories in *One-Minute Fairy Tales* are so short that they leave out much of the richness of the tales. *Tell Me a Fairy Tale*, on the other hand, offers the complete story and leaves it up to the parent how to tell it. It's a matter of preference.

Finally, there's a book on the market called *Tell Me a Story* (by Chase Collins, $8.95, 180 pages, paper, Houghton Mifflin, 1992). This book devotes itself to telling parents how to tell a story. It achieves its purpose well, but most parents need to know more than just how to tell the story—they need the substance of the fairy stories as well. *Tell Me a Fairy Tale* is almost entirely made up of the specific plots and details of the stories themselves. It devotes about ten pages to the mechanics of story telling, which is sufficient for most parents'—and children's—needs.

Contents

Introduction:

How to tell a fairy tale; how to modify a fairy tale—shorten it, lengthen it, personalize it.

The Stories:

Aladdin

Androcles and the Lion

Ashputtel

Beauty and the Beast

Between the Fiddler and the Dancer

Br'er Rabbit

Casperl

Cinderella

Damon and Pythias

Daniel in the Lion's Den

Goldilocks

Hansel and Gretel

Jack and the Beanstalk

John Henry

Johnny Appleseed

Johnny Cake

Little Red Riding Hood

Noah's Ark

Paul Bunyan

Pinocchio

Puss in Boots

Rapunzel

Romeo and Juliet

Rumpelstiltskin

Scheherazade

Sir Gawain and
the Green Knight

Sleeping Beauty

Snow White

The Dreamer

The Elves and
the Shoemaker

The Emperor's
New Clothes

The Frog Prince

The House on the Hill

The Little Bird Grows

The Little Engine that Could

The Little Scarred One

The Lost Half-Hour

The Princess and the Pea

The Snow Queen

The Sorcerer's Apprentice

The Three Little Pigs

The Tin Soldier

The Tortoise and the Hare

The Tug of War between
the Elephant and
the Whale

The Twelve Dancing
Princesses

The Ugly Duckling

The Valiant Little Tailor

Three Billy Goats Gruff

Thumbalina

Two of Everything

Appendix

Where to find full-length children's stories.

Sample Material: Introduction; Two Stories

Excerpt from the Introduction

One of the first things you discover when you read or tell fairy tales to your child is that many are frightening—or so they seem to us. Take *Rumpelstiltskin,* for example. In this story a poor miller, seeking favor with the king, promises the king that his daughter can spin straw into gold. The king seizes the daughter and tells her that she must perform this feat or she will be killed in the morning. The dwarf magician Rumpelstiltskin appears, making the gold spinning possible, but he exacts a grave price from the daughter—her firstborn child. Well, as with most fairy tales, *Rumpelstiltskin* has a happy ending, and that's part of the point, too.

Yet children don't seem scared by these tales, or if they do, they don't reveal their fear. Psychologists explain this behavior in a number of ways, none of which are terribly relevant to the telling of fairy tales.*

When you tell a story using *Tell Me a Fairy Tale* you can make it as frightening or benign as you (and your child) want it to be. Let's look at *Rumpelstiltskin* again. In the G-rated version, the miller, who recognizes that the kingdom is poor (suffering a major trade imbalance perhaps), tells the king that his daughter can turn straw into gold. The king, somewhat disbelieving, agrees that the daughter can try. Rumpelstiltskin, offers to perform this magic for the daughter—for a price. When the king finds out about the dreadful bargain the magician attempted to strike, he banishes Rumpelstiltskin and marries the daughter because she tried.

See what you can do if you don't stick to the prescribed plot? Another option is to turn out-of-date fairy tales into less sexist or less stereotyped stories, if you prefer. For example, instead of having the fair maiden waiting to be rescued by the handsome prince, she can be plotting and attempting her escape.

With *Goldilocks* I like to change the ending, so that when Goldilocks is discovered sleeping in baby bear's bed, instead of jumping up, scared, and running all the way home, she yawns and stretches, and says, "Oh, but I'm so very tired. Can't I just sleep right here?" The bear family agrees, and she curls up and

---

*But since I mentioned it, here goes: Children subconsciously fear that their parents will die and leave them. Telling children about scary things, and then showing them that there are happy endings, soothes their anxieties.

goes right back to napping comfortably in the baby bear's bed. My daughter, Karen, insists on completing Goldilocks with the "nap" even if I forget—and then puts her head down on the pillow.

Some of the stories in *Tell Me a Fairy Tale* lack the exhaustive detail of the full-blown story, so feel free to add as many details as you want. Describe clothes, shoes, hats, houses, rooms, sounds, what the characters look like, gardens, individual trees, pictures on the walls, food on the table, window coverings, smells, the sky that day—let your own imagination be your guide. Is the house big, the air cool, the leaves green or turning colors, the fireplace lit? How do the characters walk, smile, sound? Is the house made of wood or stone, and is it covered with ivy? You get the idea. Add dialogue, too. Make up the words—after all, the original storytellers did. Feel free, of course, to incorporate elements of your child's life into the tale—your daughter's name, your son's clothes, for example.

Most of all, keep an eye on your child. Vary the rhythm of the story as needed. If your child is falling asleep, by all means, continue talking about the colors, shapes, smells of the objects in the rooms—these kind of details help summon dreamtime. If your son or daughter loves animals (what child doesn't?), then add more critters to your version than there were in the original. If your child isn't excited about cleaning his or her room, maybe some of the characters in your stories clean up a lot.

Some tales are best told in the present tense, others in the past. Use what best suits your inclinations.

In *Tell Me a Fairy Tale* you'll find a wide variety of fairy tales, including the classics—Grimm, Hans Christian Andersen, Mother Goose. There are also some Bible stories, as well as tales from other cultures. These lesser-known stories are a good way of acquainting your child with other cultures, not to mention providing more entertainment.

Many fairy tales and fables don't make a whole lot of sense to adults. The plots don't hold together, the characters motivations aren't credible. So what? The stories do make sense to children.

In many of the original stories, characters do not have names. So create your own.

Magic is the principle ingredient in all fairy tales. Don't skimp here. Children have no trouble believing, and the more magic, the more fun.

You are the storyteller, which makes you a central character in each story. Change the pitch of your voice to talk like an old woman, talk like a pixie, talk like a child, even talk like an animal (for example, the lion in *Androcles and the Lion* could speak in a growly roar of a voice). Vary the rhythm of your words. Be out of breath when it's called for; speak quietly or loudly as the role requires. Sound effects—whistling, foot stomping, a clap, a gasp, snapping a finger—may be part of the story, too.

Finally, remember that every fairy tale usually begins, "Once upon a time...."

Rapunzel

Summary

Rapunzel is the story of a child raised by an evil witch, who grows long, beautiful hair. Rapunzel lives in a tower; the only way into the tower is to climb Rapunzel's hair. Rapunzel sees nobody but the witch until a prince wanders by one day and climbs up her hair. The witch punishes Rapunzel, and later the prince is hurt falling from the tower; but eventually the prince and Rapunzel find each other and live happily every after.

The Characters

Rapunzel's mother

Wants a child, and after many years becomes pregnant. Enigmatically, she covets a vegetable growing in the witch's garden called a rapunzel. (Is this the witch's doing?) Her need for the rapunzel is so great that she becomes pale and weak.

Rapunzel's father

Also wants a child badly. Yields to his wife's entreaties. Both the mother and father disappear from the story shortly after Rapunzel is born.

The Witch

An evil, mysterious character with the classic, repulsive look of a witch. Her source of income isn't revealed, but her powers seem limited only by her inclinations. Despite her evil, there is a hint of loneliness and pity about her—she wants Rapunzel to love her. In some versions, called Mother Gothel by Rapunzel.

Rapunzel

The star of the story. It's never known how Rapunzel's hair becomes so long—perhaps it's genetic, perhaps a consequence of the witch's powers. Rapunzel is beautiful and lonely, lonelier even than the witch. How Rapunzel occupies her day isn't clear; perhaps braiding and unbraiding her hair is a full-time occupation.

The Prince

The king's son. Handsome and valiant, like all princes. Not much substance, so the prince's character and looks can be embellished as much as you like.

The Plot

A husband and wife long for a child, and after many years the wife becomes pregnant.

The couple live in a house adjacent to a witch's house. From their house they can see the witch's garden, which is surrounded by a high wall.

The wife becomes enchanted, almost enthralled, with the rapunzel, an unusual leafy vegetable, growing in the witch's garden; she grows pale and weak because she cannot have the rapunzel. Finally the husband, afraid for his wife's health, goes into the witch's garden, gathers some rapunzel, and makes a salad for her.

When the witch finds out (you expected she wouldn't?), she threatens to cast a terrible spell on the husband and wife. Only by promising the witch their child do they avoid the spell.

The parents name the child Rapunzel; almost immediately afterwards they are forced to give Rapunzel up to the witch. When Rapunzel is twelve, she is made to live alone in a tower in the forest. Over the years, Rapunzel grows the longest, most beautiful hair in the world. Rapunzel herself becomes the most beautiful woman in the world. The only way up to her room in the tower is by climbing up her hair, which she must braid to make possible. That's how the witch brings food and other necessities.

"Rapunzel, Rapunzel, let down your long hair/and I will climb up the golden stair" is the witch's rhymed request.

One day a prince wanders by. He hears Rapunzel singing in her room and becomes captivated. So he hides near the tower and overhears as the witch commands, "Rapunzel, Rapunzel, let down your long hair."

The next night he visits Rapunzel. When he climbs up to Rapunzel's room, she is frightened, because she has never seen a man before. But the prince is kind and Rapunzel decides she wants to marry him. The prince visits many times more.

The witch is unaware of the prince's visits until Rapunzel innocently asks the witch why she is so much heavier climbing up her braid than the prince. Angered, the witch cuts off Rapunzel's hair, and banishes her to the wilderness.

When the prince comes to visit again, he climbs up the braid, but the witch is at the other end. The prince, in grief, leaps from the tower. He is not killed but is blinded by landing on thorns.

The prince wanders aimlessly through the world for many years. Finally he hears that sweet, familiar voice. It is Rapunzel, who hugs the prince and weeps on him. Her tears touch the prince's eyes, instantly curing him of his blindness. They live happily ever after.

How to Tell the Story

Rapunzel can be shortened by skipping ahead twelve years: Rapunzel, captured by a witch, imprisoned in the tower of a castle, is a fair beginning.

Or you can embellish the story: The witch's castle is cold and dark. Paintings of witch ancestors cover the walls. (Where do witches come from, anyway?) Preface the prince's appearance with some background about his life—perhaps he is a hunter, perhaps a skilled tracker of game (which tells what he was doing when he happened to come across the tower hidden in the forest). You could bring the parents back into the story, too. Perhaps they didn't just give up on their lost daughter but went to the court to beseech the prince to find her—and he did.

Because the story takes place over many years, you have the opportunity to fill in the missing time with details. Tell how the witch raised Rapunzel, how she got her hair to grow six stories long. Make up the words to the spell the witch could have used. Pretend you're using it to make your own daughter's hair grow long. It's all up to you and your child.

The Elves and the Shoemaker

Summary

This is a story about a poor shoemaker who ran out of material from which to make shoes. Magically, new shoes appear in his shop overnight. This happens again and again. When the shoemaker and his wife stay awake all night to see what's up, they find two naked elves working hard. The shoemaker decides to make the elves little suits of clothes. The elves put on the clothes and then are never seen again, but the shoemaker is left with good luck.

The Characters

The Shoemaker

A kindly, elderly man, who's lately been having bad luck. Through no fault of his own, his business isn't going well, and he can't afford the material he needs to make shoes to sell.

The Shoemaker's Wife

Also a kindly person. She helps the shoemaker sell shoes.

The Elves

Tiny beings with implied magical powers and fantastic shoemaking skills. It's unclear how they came to know about the shoemaker's problems. The elves wear no clothing.

The Customers

A small cast of characters who wish the shoemaker well. They would like to buy shoes from his shop, if only he had something to offer.

The Plot

As the story begins, the shoemaker has become poorer and poorer over the years. Now he only has enough leather to make one more pair of shoes.

He plans to do the best he can with the material at hand, and he cuts a pattern. But it's late and his only candle has burned out, so he goes to bed. When he gets up in the morning, he finds the pair of shoes finished—and perfectly, too.

A customer walks into the shop and buys the shoes. With that money, the shoemaker purchases material for two more pairs of shoes. He cuts patterns for those shoes, and goes to bed, planning on sewing the shoes in the morning.

In the morning, two more beautiful pairs of shoes have been made. The shoemaker sells the shoes at a high price. Now the shoemaker has money to buy material for four pairs of shoes.

As before, he cuts four patterns and goes to bed. Next morning, there are four finished pairs of shoes—and the customers immediately snap them up.

And so the process continues, and, in short order, the shoemaker becomes a wealthy man.

One night the shoemaker and his wife decide to stay awake to see how this miracle is happening. They see two elves, hard at work—but the elves wear no clothes. As soon as the elves are finished making the shoes, they vanish.

To thank the elves, the shoemaker and his wife make some tiny clothes for them. The shoemaker and his wife are worried because it's cold outside and the elves have no clothes. They work diligently to make the tiny shirts, pants, caps, coats, socks, and, of course, two pairs of tiny shoes.

When the elves return, instead of patterns for shoes, they find the clothes. They put on the clothes with delight and sing a song: "Now that we're boys so fine and neat/Why cobble more for others' feet?"

The elves never return, but the shoemaker and his wife continue to prosper and have good luck for the rest of their lives.

How to Tell the Story

Your child may be curious about what the shoes looked like. Probably not like Nikes or Velcro Stride Rites. But they might have been children's shoes!

Also, it's possible that the shoemaker let the process continue for a few days or months before staying up to find out what was happening. Perhaps the shoemaker left out some cookies in the interim. One version of the fairy tale has the shoemaker staying up not long before Christmas and leaving the clothes out on Christmas Eve.

Add dialogue between the shoemaker and his wife. Was it her curiosity that prompted the decision to stay awake and watch? You might also be inclined to mention the shoemaker's children—they're much too young to help their parents out, but they giggle and squeal with delight to learn that elves have been night-time visitors. Maybe the children are the ones to suggest rewarding the elves with a gift. Then there's the matter of the elves dancing about the shoemaker's shop: You could really have a good time describing that scene.

You can also make up a lot about the elves. What do they look like? Where do they come from? What does the clothing the shoemaker and his wife made look like? Tiny socks, tiny shirts, tiny pants—children love to hear about miniaturized things. Try changing the sex of one of the elves (why should they both be boys?)—but remember to rewrite their song accordingly. Now it might go something like this: "Now that we're dressed so fine and neat/Why cobble more for others' feet?"

This isn't a story you have to worry about shortening; it can be told very quickly when you'd like your child to go right to bed.

About the Author

Bill Adler, Jr. is the president of Adler & Robin Books, Inc., a literary agency and book packaging company. He is one of the very few agents in the country who is also a bestselling author.

Among the dozen-plus books he has written are several on parenting and activities for children. Some of Adler's books include: *Baby-English: A Dictionary for Interpreting the Secret Language of Toddlers* (with Karen Adler, age two, Pocket Books); *Outwitting Toddlers* (Lowell House); *Ask Me Something I Don't Know* (with Beth Pratt-Dewey, Avon); *Outwitting Squirrels: 101 Cunning Stratagems to Reduce Dramatically the Egregious Misappropriation of Seed from Your Bird Feeder by Squirrels* (Chicago Review Press); *Outwitting Critters* (Lyons and Burford); *Outwitting the Neighbors* (Simon & Schuster); *The Home Remodeler's Combat Manual* (HarperCollins); *The Weather*

Sourcebook (with Ron Wagner, Globe Pequot); and *The Non-Smoker's Bill of Rights* (with Steve Allen, William Morrow and Company). *Outwitting Critters* was a Literary Guild selection and a Book of the Month Club gardening club selection.

Of all his books, Adler's favorite is *Outwitting Squirrels,* not just because it was a treat to write but because it became such a success—even after twenty publishers turned the proposal down. While reviewing this book *USA Today* called Adler, "a trendspotter." *The Wall Street Journal* called the book "a master-piece," and the book was twice enthusiastically reviewed in *The New York Times* and *The Washington Post.* Talk show host Rosie O'Donnell told her viewers, "Bill Adler is my hero. I love this book. Go buy this book."

Outwitting Squirrels is not only a testament to the cunning and perseverance of squirrels, it is a testament to Bill Adler's creative insight into the book business. The book has gone into printing after printing, and now the number of copies sold exceeds 250,000. *Regardie's Magazine* had this to say: "Adler still feeds the birds, but now he also squirrels away royalties."

Manuscript Details

Length: approximately 250 manuscript pages/50 to 70 stories

Illustrations: one for each story

Time to delivery: eight months

Acknowledgments

As with any book, there are numerous hands involved in making it a success. First and foremost, Peggy Robin worked long and hard to repair many mistakes I made in early drafts and contributed many useful sections. A million kudos to Tracy Quinn, editor extraordinaire, for her help. Jessica Allen also helped make this book come to pass. Thanks, too, to Gail Rebhan for her great artwork, Patricia Borthwick for copyediting, and Cindy Peters for her design expertise. Vicki McCullough and everyone else at Independent Publishers Group were instrumental in making this book happen.

I also want to thank those authors and editors who provided valuable insights: Toni Sciarra, Wendy Hubbert, John Bell, Judy Brief, Laurie Abkemeier, Linda Matthews, Cynthia Sherry, Linda Reagan, Melissa Rosati, Kathy Welton, Gene Brissie, Martha O'Sullivan, Charles Inlander, Deborah Brody, Ken Lawrence, Larry Kahaner, and Katie Tamony.

About Bill Adler, Jr.

Bill Adler, Jr. is the president of Adler & Robin Books, Inc. (www.adlerbooks.com), a literary agency and book packaging company. Adler is one of the most creative agents in the country—after all, there are perhaps at most one or two agents who are themselves bestselling authors.

Adler & Robin Books, Inc., represents general nonfiction and computer and technology books.

During his free time, Bill Adler flies airplanes. Adler is an aerobatic pilot who flies loops, rolls, and other maneuvers in a Pitts Special and was recently seen flying on the television show, *Hard Copy.*

Adler received his B.A. from Wesleyan University, where he majored in government and did graduate work in organic chemistry. He received his M.A. from Columbia University's School of International Affairs, specializing in Soviet foreign policy, a field that is now ancient history. In the early 1980s, Adler was a congressional lobbyist on defense and foreign policy and then a political consultant. His study on nuclear breeder reactors was published in *The Congressional Record.* He also served as a member of the U.S. Delegation to the U.N. Commission on Human Rights in 1978.

He lives in Washington, D.C., with his wife, Peggy Robin, also a multi-talented writer, and cofounder of Adler & Robin Books, Inc. They have a daughter, Karen, whose first book, *Baby-English,* was published in 1993 on Karen's third birthday. Their second child, Claire, has not yet written a book.

Adler is the author of more than a dozen books, including several parenting and children's books. Some of Adler's books include *Outwitting Squirrels: 101 Cunning Stratagems to Reduce Dramatically the Egregious Misappropriation of Seed from Your Bird Feeder by Squirrels* (Chicago Review Press), *The Home Remodeler's Combat Manual* (HarperCollins), *Ask Me Something I Don't Know* (with Beth Pratt-Dewey, Avon Books), *The Weather Sourcebook* (with Ron Wagner, Globe Pequot), *The Non-Smoker's Bill of Rights* (with Steve Allen, William Morrow and Company), *Baby-English: A Dictionary for Interpreting the Secret Language of Toddlers* (with Karen Adler, age two, Pocket Books), *Tell Me a Fairy Tale* (E.P. Dutton), *Outwitting Toddlers* (with Peggy Robin, Lowell House), *Outwitting Critters* (Lyons and Burford), and *Outwitting the Neighbors* (Simon & Schuster). *Outwitting Critters* was a Literary Guild selection and a Book of the Month Club selection for their gardening club.

Of all his books, Adler's favorite is *Outwitting Squirrels,* not just because it was a treat to write but because it became such a success—even after twenty publishers turned the proposal down. While reviewing this book *USA Today* called Adler "a trendspotter." *The Wall Street Journal* called the book "a masterpiece." The book was twice enthusiastically reviewed in *The New York Times* and *The Washington Post.* Talk show host and bird feeder Rosie O'Donnell said, "Bill Adler is my hero. I love this book. Go buy this book."

Outwitting Squirrels is not only a testament to the cunning and perseverance of squirrels, it is a testament to Adler's creative insight into the book business. The book has gone into printing after printing, and now the number of copies sold exceeds 250,000. *Regardie's Magazine* had this to say about the book: "Adler still feeds the birds, but now he also squirrels away royalties." (See www.outwittingsquirrels.com.)

Here is what some reviewers have said about Adler's books:

Outwitting Squirrels

Outwitting Squirrels...ingenious tricks to keep squirrels from eating all the seed when the feeders fail.

—*The Washington Post*

In light of his entertaining, instructional, and philosophical contribution to the understanding of and possible solutions to such a universal problem, we should make Bill Adler, Jr. an honorary New Hampshirite.

—*Monadnock* (N.H.) *Ledger*

What the birdfeeders of America long have needed is a guru... I'm pleased to announce there's a new voice on the front lines of birdfeeding. His name is Bill Adler, Jr.... Adler assembled his findings into a nifty volume entitled *Outwitting Squirrels*.

—*Minneapolis Star Tribune*

A fascinating book.

—*Tuscaloosa News*

Bill Adler, Jr., a writer in Washington, has just published a treatise titled *Outwitting Squirrels...* [His stratagems are] particularly appealing.

—*The New York Times*

At last! A book that addresses life's really important issue, or, in any case, the issue most crucial to people who like to feed birds.

—*Detroit Free Press*

A masterpiece of squirrel stratagems.

—*The Wall Street Journal*

An excellent book...both entertainingly witty and extremely helpful. A must.

—*The Ottawa Citizen*

I learned a lot from Bill Adler.

—*The Toronto Star*

Impeccable Birdfeeding

The author of *Outwitting Squirrels* strikes again.

—*The Milwaukee Journal Sentinel*

The most entertaining backyard birding book we know! Bill Adler, Jr., author of *Outwitting Squirrels,* needs no introduction to bird lovers. He's simply the funniest, most practical writer on birdfeeding.

—The Nature Company

Perspective makes this book different: Mr. Adler puts the needs of the hobbyist before those of the birds.

—*The Dallas Morning News*

The advice he delivers is supremely practical, his style spare and straightforward and his sense of humor is enlivening throughout the book. This is an eminently readable book, perhaps the only one the amateur bird-feeding hobbyist needs on his shelf.

—*The Washington Post*

This book will add greatly to a person's enjoyment of birdfeeding.

—*The St. Louis Post-Dispatch*

Outwitting Critters

Adler tells engaging stories, many bordering on suburban legend. *Outwitting Critters* surfeits with interesting facts and horse-sense hints.

—*The Village Voice*

Adler has the answers, and they are creative as well as non-toxic.

—*Chicago Tribune*

He offers...comprehensive treatment of the subject and provides recommendations that are grounded in common sense.

—Library Journal

The Outwitting Series by Bill Adler, Jr.

Conceived in 1988, the *Outwitting* books have been a incredible success, receiving excellent reviews and topping everyone's expectations for sales. Created by author and literary agent Bill Adler, Jr., the *Outwitting* books are a reminder that there's still a great deal of talent and imagination in book publishing. Adler proves that you can combine great ideas with books that provide practical, easy-to-use solutions to life's everyday problems. From squirrels to home contractors, Adler has the answers.

Outwitting Squirrels
101 Cunning Stratagems to Reduce Dramatically the Egregious Misappropriation of Seed From Your Birdfeeder by Squirrels
($12.95)

"Bill Adler, Jr. is my hero. I love this book. Go buy this book."
—Rosie O'Donnell

Outwitting Critters
A Surefire Manual for Confronting Devious Animals and Winning
($12.95)

"Adler tells engaging stories, many bordering on suburban legend. *Outwitting Critters* surfeits with interesting facts and horse-sense hints."

—The Village Voice

Outwitting Toddlers
And Other Small Human Beings
($12.95)

"This book saved my sanity."

—Jane G., Tulsa, Oklahoma

Outwitting Home Contractors

Dealing with People Who Are Supposed to Make Your House Wonderful, but Who Have One Thought on Their Minds—"When's Miller Time?" (Formerly titled, *The Home Remodeler's Combat Manual.*) *($9.95)*

> "Practical, hands-on advice for anyone and everyone who's remodeling their house or apartment."
>
> —Jason T., Rockville, MD

Outwitting the Neighbors

A Practical and Entertaining Guide to Achieving Peaceful Coexistence with the People Next Door
($11.00)

> "A witty paperback."
>
> —*Indianapolis Star*

Coming soon:
Outwitting Your Appetite, Outwitting Microsoft Windows, Outwitting Your Teenager, Outwitting Traffic, Outwitting Deer, and *Outwitting Fish.*